Selected Natural Attenuation Monitoring Data, Operable Unit 1, Naval Undersea Warfare Center, Division Keyport, Washington, 2007 and 2008

By R.S. Dinicola and R.L. Huffman

Prepared in cooperation with
Department of the Navy, Naval Facilities Engineering Command, Northwest

Open-File Report 2009–1141

U.S. Department of the Interior
U.S. Geological Survey

U.S. Department of the Interior
KEN SALAZAR, Secretary

U.S. Geological Survey
Suzette M. Kimball, Acting Director

U.S. Geological Survey, Reston, Virginia: 2009

For more information on the USGS—the Federal source for science about the Earth, its natural and living resources, natural hazards, and the environment, visit http://www.usgs.gov or call 1-888-ASK-USGS

For an overview of USGS information products, including maps, imagery, and publications, visit http://www.usgs.gov/pubprod

To order this and other USGS information products, visit http://store.usgs.gov

Contents

Abstract..1
Introduction...2
    Purpose and Scope 2
Sample Collection and Analysis...7
Natural Attenuation Monitoring Data...8
    Geochemical Data and Predominant Redox Conditions 8
    Volatile Organic Compounds..10
        Volatile Organic Compound Concentrations Beneath the Phytoremediation
            Plantations...10
        Volatile Organic Compound Concentrations in the Intermediate Aquifer......................10
Summary...11
Acknowledgments 12
References Cited...12
Appendix A. Quality Assurance and Control of U.S. Geological Survey 2007 and 2008
        Geochemical Sampling 42

Figures

Figure 1. Map showing location of the Operable Unit 1 study area, Naval Undersea
          Warfare Center, Division Keyport, Washington 3
Figure 2. Map showing location of former landfill, two phytoremediation plantations,
          and data collection sites at Operable Unit 1, Naval Undersea Warfare Center,
          Division Keyport, Washington 6

Tables

Table 1. Wells and piezometers sampled and groundwater levels measured at
         Operable Unit 1, Naval Undersea Warfare Center, Division Keyport,
         Washington, June 2007 and June 2008 4
Table 2. Predominant redox conditions at wells and piezometers, and groundwater
         geochemical data collected at Operable Unit 1, Naval Undersea Warfare
         Center, Division Keyport, Washington, 1996 to 2008 14
Table 3. Concentrations of selected volatile organic compounds in groundwater
         samples from monitoring wells and piezometers collected by the U.S.
         Geological Survey at Operable Unit 1, Naval Undersea Warfare Center,
         Division Keyport, Washington., 1999–2008.. 30

Conversion Factors, Datums, and Abbreviations and Acronyms

Conversion Factors

Multiply	By	To obtain
acre	4,047	square meter (m^2)
acre	0.4047	hectare (ha)
foot (ft)	0.3048	meter (m)

Temperature in degrees Celsius (°C) may be converted to degrees Fahrenheit (°F) as follows:

$$°F=(1.8×°C)+32.$$

Specific conductance is given in microsiemens per centimeter at 25 degrees Celsius (µS/cm at 25°C).

Concentrations of chemical constituents in water are given either in milligrams per liter (mg/L) or micrograms per liter (µg/L).

Datums

Vertical coordinate information is referenced to the North American Vertical Datum of 1988 (NAVD 88).

Horizontal coordinate information is referenced to the North American Datum of 1927 (NAD 27).

Altitude, as used in this report, refers to distance above the vertical datum.

Abbreviations and Acronyms

1,1-DCA	1,1-dichloroethane
1,1-DCE	1,1-dichloroethene
BTEX	benzene, toluene, ethylbenzene, xylenes
CA	chloroethane
cis-DCE	*cis*-1,2-dichloroethene
CO_2	carbon dioxide
DO	dissolved oxygen
DOC	dissolved organic carbon
H_2	dissolved hydrogen
nM	nanoMolar
NUWC	Naval Undersea Warfare Center
NWQL	National Water Quality Laboratory (USGS)
ORP	oxidation-reduction potential
OU	Operable Unit
RSKSOP	Robert S. Kerr Standard Operating Procedure
Redox	reduction/oxidation
TA	TestAmerica Laboratories
TCA	1,1,1-trichloroethane
TCE	trichloroethene
USEPA	U.S. Environmental Protection Agency
USGS	U.S. Geological Survey
VC	vinyl chloride
VOC	volatile organic compound
YSI	Yellow Springs Instruments

Selected Natural Attenuation Monitoring Data, Operable Unit 1, Naval Undersea Warfare Center, Division Keyport, Washington, 2007 and 2008

By R.S. Dinicola and R.L. Huffman

Abstract

Previous investigations indicate that natural attenuation and biodegradation of chlorinated volatile organic compounds (VOCs) are substantial in groundwater beneath the 9-acre former landfill at Operable Unit 1 (OU 1), Naval Undersea Warfare Center, Division Keyport, Washington. Phytoremediation combined with on-going natural attenuation processes was the preferred remedy selected by the Navy, as specified in the Record of Decision for the site. The Navy planted two hybrid poplar plantations on the landfill in spring 1999 to remove and to control the migration of chlorinated VOCs in shallow groundwater. The U.S. Geological Survey (USGS) has continued to monitor groundwater geochemistry to ensure that conditions remain favorable for contaminant biodegradation as specified in the Record of Decision. In this report are groundwater geochemical and selected VOC data collected at OU 1 by the USGS during June 18–21, 2007, and June 16–18, 2008, in support of long-term monitoring for natural attenuation.

For 2007 and 2008, strongly reducing conditions (sulfate reduction and methanogenesis) most favorable for reductive dechlorination of VOCs were inferred for 9 of 16 upper-aquifer wells and piezometers in the northern and southern phytoremediation plantations. Predominant redox conditions in groundwater from the intermediate aquifer just downgradient from the landfill remained mildly reducing and somewhat favorable for reductive dechlorination of VOCs. Dissolved hydrogen (H_2) concentrations measured in the upper aquifer during 2007 and 2008 generally have been lower than H_2 concentrations measured before 2002. However, widespread and relatively high methane and sulfide concentrations indicate that the lower H_2 concentrations measured do not support a trend from strongly to mildly reducing redox conditions because no widespread changes in groundwater redox conditions were identified that should result in less favorable conditions for the reductive dechlorination of the chlorinated VOCs.

For the upper aquifer beneath the northern phytoremediation plantation, chlorinated VOC concentrations in 2007 and 2008 at most piezometers were similar to or slightly less than chlorinated VOC concentrations measured in previous years. The only chlorinated VOC positively detected at piezometers P1-1 and P1-5 was cis-1,2-dichloroethene (cis-DCE); most chlorinated VOC concentrations at piezometer P1-3 were at the lowest levels since monitoring began in 1999. Most VOC concentrations at piezometer P1-4 were similar to VOC concentrations measured in previous years except that vinyl chloride (VC) concentrations inexplicably increased from 280 micrograms per liter (μg/L) in June 2007 to 750 μg/L in June 2008. In 2008, measurement of the sum of concentrations of ethane and ethene, reductive dechlorination byproducts, was at the highest level at most northern plantation wells and piezometers, which is evidence of reductive dechlorination of chlorinated VOCs.

For the upper aquifer beneath the southern phytoremediation plantation, chlorinated VOC concentrations in 2007 and 2008 at the piezometers were most often extremely high and they continued to vary considerable over space and between years. At piezometer P1-6, the total chlorinated VOC concentration increased from 380 μg/L in 2007 to more than 20,000 μg/L in 2008. At piezometer P1-7 in 2008, the concentrations of trichloroethene, cis-DCE, and VC were the highest to date, but total chlorinated VOC concentrations at piezometers P1-8, P1-9, and P1-10 in 2008 were relatively low compared to historical levels. The magnitude and persistence of chlorinated VOC concentrations indicate that non-aqueous phase liquid chloroethenes likely are beneath the southern plantation, and the temporal variability in concentrations likely is a result of variations in precipitation and groundwater levels interacting with the non-aqueous phase liquid. The reductive dechlorination byproducts ethane and ethene were detected at all wells and piezometers in the southern plantation, which is reliable evidence of reductive dechlorination of dissolved VOCs.

For the intermediate aquifer, total chlorinated VOC concentrations in 2008 at wells MW1-25, MW1-28, and MW1-39 were consistent with concentrations from previous years. However, concentrations of VC at these wells in 2008 were the highest measured to date, as were the sum of concentrations of ethane and ethene measured at wells MW1-25 and MW1-28. These data suggest that either the rate of reductive dechlorination of *cis*-DCE to create VC may have increased, or more non-aqueous phase liquid has dissolved into groundwater.

Introduction

Chlorinated volatile organic compounds (VOCs) are in groundwater beneath the 9-acre former landfill at Operable Unit 1 (OU 1) at the Naval Undersea Warfare Center (NUWC), Division Keyport. The NUWC is on a small peninsula in Kitsap County, Washington, in an extension of Puget Sound called Liberty Bay (fig. 1). The former landfill is on the narrow strip of land connecting the peninsula to the mainland and is adjacent to tidal flats that are an extension of Liberty and Dogfish Bays. The OU 1 landfill was constructed in a former marshland and is unlined at the bottom. The landfill was the primary disposal area for domestic and industrial wastes generated by NUWC Division Keyport from the 1930s through 1973. The landfill received paints, thinners, solvents, acids, dried sludge from a wastewater-treatment plant, and other industrial wastes. The most concentrated disposal area for waste paints and solvents was at the southern end of the landfill.

Groundwater beneath OU 1 is within a series of aquifers that are composed of permeable sand, gravel, or fill materials separated by finer grained silt or clay layers. Volatile organic compound contamination at OU 1 is only in about the top 60 ft of the unconsolidated deposits in the four hydrogeologic units: the unsaturated zone, the upper aquifer, the middle aquitard, and the intermediate aquifer. Groundwater in the unconfined upper aquifer generally flows from the east to the west toward Dogfish Bay. Groundwater in the predominately confined intermediate aquifer flows toward the landfill from the south and from the west, and then flows northwest beneath the landfill toward Dogfish Bay (Dinicola and others, 2002). Two perennial freshwater creeks drain the marsh adjacent to the landfill and discharge into the tide flats of Dogfish Bay.

Chlorinated VOCs are in the upper and intermediate aquifers and in surface water at OU 1. The predominant contaminants in groundwater beneath OU 1 are trichloroethene (TCE) and degradation byproducts *cis*-1,2-dichloroethene

(*cis*-DCE) and vinyl chloride (VC). The compound 1,1,1-trichloroethane (TCA) and degradation byproducts 1,1-dichloroethane (1,1-DCA), 1,1-dichloroethene (1,1-DCE), and chloroethane (CA) have been detected at concentrations of concern at a few locations at OU 1. A need for remedial action was identified because these hazardous compounds are a potential risk to humans (URS Consultants, Inc., 1998). Phytoremediation combined with on-going natural attenuation processes was the preferred remedy selected by the Navy, as specified in the Record of Decision for the site (URS Consultants, Inc., 1998). The Navy planted two hybrid poplar plantations on the landfill (fig. 2) in spring 1999 to remove and control the migration of chlorinated VOCs in shallow groundwater (URS Greiner, Inc., 1999). The landfill between the plantations is covered with pavement, although the area north of the northern plantation is permeable.

Purpose and Scope

The Navy began a cooperative effort with the U.S. Geological Survey (USGS) in 1995 to investigate various natural attenuation mechanisms at OU 1. Field and laboratory studies from 1996 through 2000 showed that natural attenuation and biodegradation of chlorinated VOCs in shallow groundwater at OU 1 were substantial (URS Consultants, Inc., 1997; Bradley and others, 1998; Dinicola and others, 2002). The USGS has continued to monitor the geochemistry of groundwater to ensure that conditions remain favorable for contaminant biodegradation. Annual monitoring from 2001 through 2006 confirmed biodegradation (Dinicola and Huffman, 2007). USGS data collected from 1996 through 2006 are in Dinicola and others (2002), Dinicola (2003, 2004, 2006), and Dinicola and Huffman (2004, 2006, 2007).

This report presents two sets of groundwater chemical and selected VOC data collected by the USGS at OU 1 during June 18–21, 2007 and June 16–18, 2008, in support of the long-term monitoring for natural attenuation. The USGS collected groundwater samples from 14 wells and 9 piezometers in 2007 and 2008 (table 1 and fig. 2), and concentrations of various geochemical constituents used to evaluate groundwater redox conditions were determined in all samples. Concentrations of VOCs also were determined by the USGS in samples collected from seven of nine piezometers in 2007, and in samples from all nine piezometers and three intermediate aquifer wells in 2008. The Navy determined VOC concentrations in samples they collected from other OU 1 monitoring wells during June 2007 and 2008; some of those data are discussed in this report.

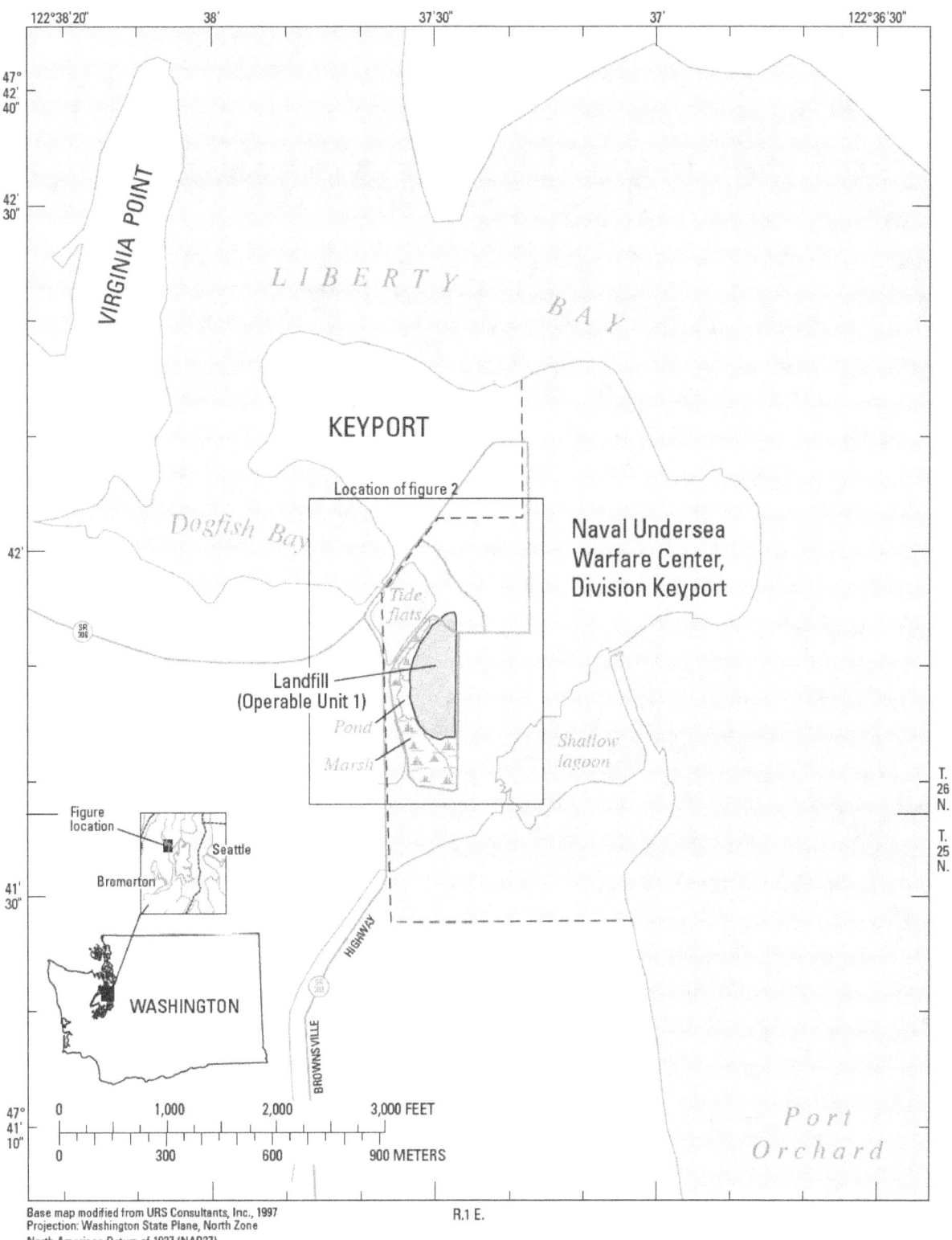

Figure 1.   Location of the Operable Unit 1 study area, Naval Undersea Warfare Center, Division Keyport, Washington.

Table 1.   Wells and piezometers sampled and groundwater levels measured at Operable Unit 1, Naval Undersea Warfare Center, Division Keyport, Washington, June 2007 and June 2008.

[**Well or piezometer site No.:** MW, monitoring well; P, piezometer; **USGS site No.:** Unique number for each site based on latitude and longitude of the site. First six digits are latitude, next seven digits are longitude, and final two digits are a sequence number to uniquely identify each site. **Altitudes of groundwater levels and measuring points** are given in feet above or below (-) NAVD88. **Groundwater level** is in feet below measuring point (bmp). **Depth of well and screened interval** are in feet below land surface. **Altitude of measuring point:** Water levels in wells are usually reported as depths below land surface, although the measuring point can be any convenient fixed place near the top of the well. For these wells and piezometers, the measuring points are marked points on the tops of well casings—they vary from being near the land surface to a few feet above land surface. The altitude of the measuring point is commonly recorded so that static water levels also can be reported as altitudes; **VOCs sampled by USGS:** Y, yes, N, no. **Abbreviations:** USGS, U.S. Geological Survey; VOC, volatile organic compound; ft, foot; ft bmp, feet below measuring point; –, not measured]

Well or piezometer site No.	USGS site No.	Date and time measured		Groundwater level altitude (ft)	Groundwater level (ft bmp)	Altitude of measuring point (ft)	Depth of well (ft)	VOCs sampled by USGS
1MW-1	474151122373201	06-19-07	16:00	3.36	6.70	10.06	16.5	N
		06-17-08	13:40	4.36	5.70			N
MW1-2	474153122373101	06-19-07	14:00	2.37	9.52	11.89	18.5	N
		06-17-08	11:20	2.25	9.64			N
MW1-3	474152122372501	06-18-07	16:50	9.30	4.25	13.55	11.5	N
		06-16-08	12:20	9.62	3.93			N
MW1-4	474145122372801	06-20-07	12:00	5.51	6.69	12.20	13.0	N
		06-18-08	14:20	5.58	6.62			N
MW1-5	474146122373201	06-20-07	16:00	4.13	8.95	13.08	12.0	N
		06-18-08	12:00	4.32	8.76			N
MW1-16	474146122372801	06-20-07	13:40	5.31	7.52	12.83	12.0	N
		06-18-08	13:15	5.49	7.34			N
MW1-17	474150122373201	06-20-07	17:30	6.12	5.82	11.94	13.5	N
		06-18-08	11:00	6.42	5.52			N
MW1-20	474145122372501	06-18-07	16:30	6.44	4.00	10.44	16.0	N
		06-18-08	13:30	6.56	3.88			N
MW1-25	474154122373201	06-18-07	14:40	1.63	10.28	11.91	49.0	N
		06-17-08	15:00	1.39	10.52			Y
MW1-28	474153122373301	06-18-07	14:40	1.61	11.49	13.10	45.0	N
		06-17-08	15:20	1.32	11.78			Y
MW1-33	474140122373201	06-18-07	12:50	10.81	.68	11.49	41.0	N
		06-16-08	12:15	10.94	.55			N
MW1-38	474156122373701	06-21-07	14:40	.80	9.03	9.83	50.0	N
		06-17-08	11:00	-.68	10.51			N

Table 1. Wells and piezometers sampled and groundwater levels measured at Operable Unit 1, Naval Undersea Warfare Center, Division Keyport, Washington, June 2007 and June 2008.—Continued

[**Well or piezometer site No.:** MW, monitoring well; P, piezometer; **USGS site No.:** Unique number for each site based on latitude and longitude of the site. First six digits are latitude, next seven digits are longitude, and final two digits are a sequence number to uniquely identify each site. **Altitudes of groundwater levels and measuring points** are given in feet above or below (-) NAVD88. **Groundwater level** is in feet below measuring point (bmp). **Depth of well and screened interval** are in feet below land surface. **Altitude of measuring point:** Water levels in wells are usually reported as depths below land surface, although the measuring point can be any convenient fixed place near the top of the well. For these wells and piezometers, the measuring points are marked points on the tops of well casings—they vary from being near the land surface to a few feet above land surface. The altitude of the measuring point is commonly recorded so that static water levels also can be reported as altitudes; **VOCs sampled by USGS:** Y, yes, N, no. **Abbreviations:** USGS, U.S. Geological Survey; VOC, volatile organic compound; ft, foot; ft bmp, feet below measuring point; –, not measured]

Well or piezometer site No.	USGS site No.	Date and time measured		Groundwater level altitude (ft)	Groundwater level (ft bmp)	Altitude of measuring point (ft)	Depth of well (ft)	VOCs sampled by USGS
MW1-39	474157122373701	06-21-07	14:30	.71	9.14	9.85	33.7	N
		06-17-08	11:10	-.80	10.65			Y
MW1-41	474152122372901	06-19-07	11:40	6.67	8.60	15.27	15.0	N
		06-16-08	14:30	6.85	8.42			N
P1-1	474153122372801	06-19-07	11:50	5.90	8.46	14.36	15.0	N
		06-16-08	14:20	5.75	8.61			Y
P1-3	474153122373102	06-19-07	13:15	3.28	9.51	12.79	15.0	Y
		06-17-08	11:00	3.52	9.27			Y
P1-4	474152122373101	06-19-07	15:00	–	–	12.55	15.0	Y
		06-16-08	15:40	4.31	8.24			Y
P1-5	474152122372801	06-19-07	14:20	6.16	8.90	15.06	15.0	N
		06-16-08	14:30	6.12	8.94			Y
P1-6	474146122373001	06-20-07	14:50	5.18	7.58	12.76	15.0	Y
		06-18-08	11:30	5.35	7.41			Y
P1-7	474145122373101	06-20-07	15:30	5.09	7.03	12.12	15.0	Y
		06-18-08	12:00	5.23	6.89			Y
P1-8	474147122372801	06-20-07	14:20	5.78	6.28	12.06	15.0	Y
		06-18-08	14:50	6.05	6.01			Y
P1-9	474145122372901	06-20-07	13:00	5.31	6.60	11.91	15.0	Y
		06-18-08	13:10	5.47	6.44			Y
P1-10	474145122372601	06-20-07	11:40	6.33	5.53	11.86	15.0	Y
		06-18-08	14:20	6.40	5.46			Y

Base map modified from URS Consultants, Inc., 1997
Projection: Washington State Plane, North Zone
North American Datum of 1927 (NAD27)

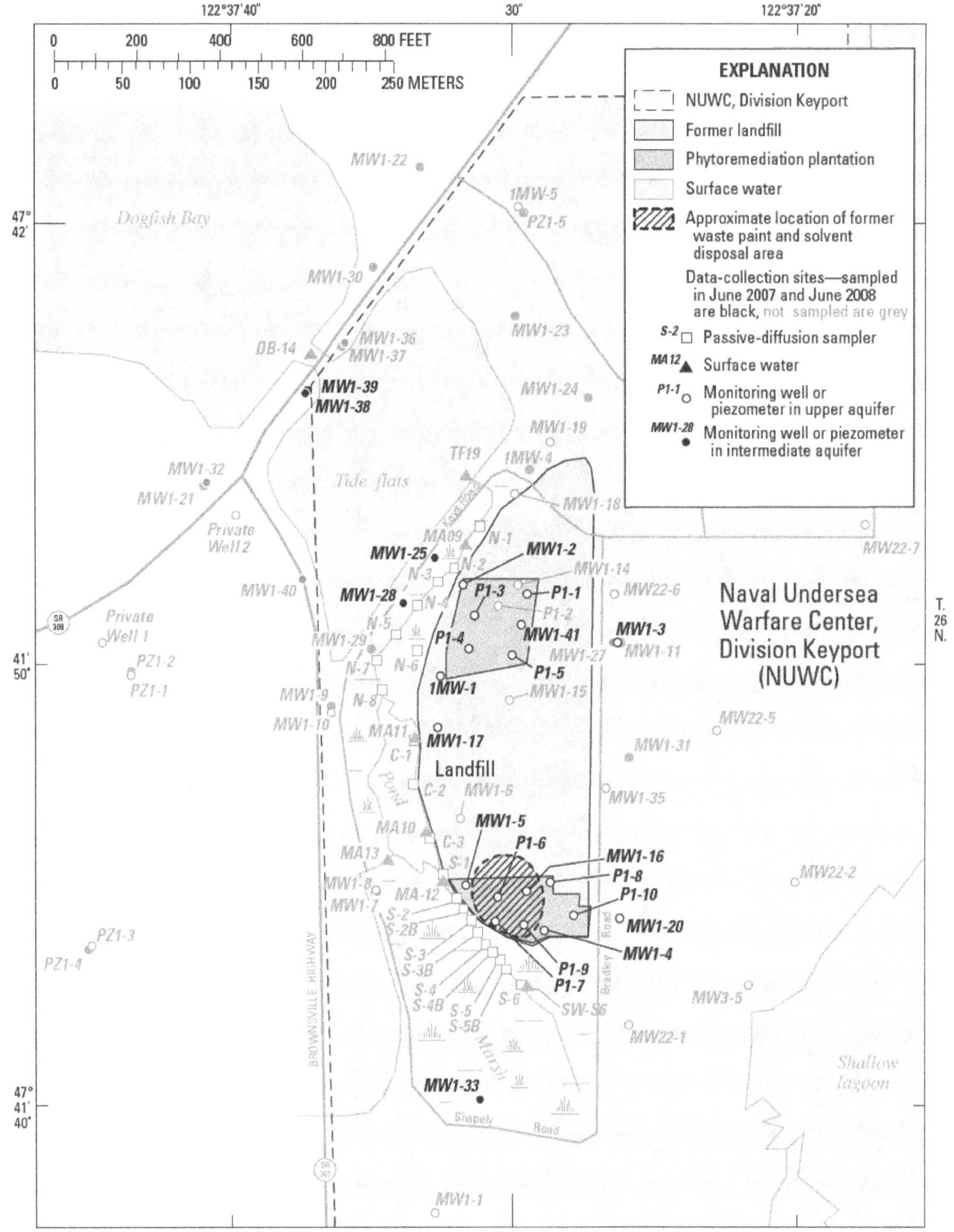

Figure 2. Location of former landfill, two phytoremediation plantations, and data collection sites at Operable Unit 1, Naval Undersea Warfare Center, Division Keyport, Washington.

Sample Collection and Analysis

Groundwater-level measurements, sample collection and processing, and field analyses were in accordance with applicable USGS procedures (U.S. Geological Survey, variously dated), except that samples were collected using a peristaltic pump. Geochemical measurements and concentrations determined for all samples included dissolved hydrogen (H_2), dissolved oxygen (DO), filtered organic carbon (referred to as dissolved organic carbon, DOC), filtered nitrate plus nitrite, filtered manganese, filtered ferrous iron (or iron (II)), filtered sulfate, unfiltered sulfide, dissolved methane, dissolved carbon dioxide, pH, specific conductance, oxidation-reduction potential (ORP), and filtered chloride. Concentrations of 64 VOCs were determined for samples from piezometers in 2007 and 2008, and from 3 wells in 2008. Concentrations of the dissolved gases ethane and ethene were determined for all samples.

After measuring depth to groundwater, all well and piezometer samples were collected with a peristaltic pump and single-use polyurethane tubing. A stainless-steel weight was attached to the bottom of the tubing to accurately collect the sample from the mid-screen altitude in each well. Samples were collected after approximately three casing-volumes of water were purged from the wells and after allowing the analytes pH, specific conductance, and DO to stabilize within 0.1 unit, 5 percent, and 0.3 mg/L, respectively. Those three analytes and ORP were measured in a flow-through chamber using temperature-compensated sensors from a Yellow Springs Instruments (YSI) data sonde. The specific conductance sensor was checked daily with standard reference solutions; the pH sensor was calibrated daily with two pH standards; and the DO sensor was calibrated daily using the water-saturated air method and occasionally verified with zero DO solution. Dissolved-oxygen analyses were confirmed for most samples using 0 to 1 mg/L CHEMets Rhodazine-D colorimetric ampoules (manufactured by CHEMetrics, Inc., Calverton, Virginia). These ampoules were filled directly from the sampling tube after well purging was completed.

Concentrations of iron (II) were measured in the field in samples that had been filtered through a 0.45-μm membrane filter using a colorimetric 1,10 phenanthroline indicator method and a Hach Model 2010 spectrophotometer following Hach Method 8146 (Hach Company, 1998; adapted from American Public Health Association, 1980). Sulfide concentrations were immediately measured in the field using a colorimetric methylene-blue indicator method using the same spectrophotometer according to Hach Method 8131 (Hach Company, 1998; procedure is equivalent to U.S. Environmental Protection Agency (USEPA) method 376.2 (U.S. Environmental Protection Agency,

1983)). Methodologies used to determine iron and sulfide concentrations also are described online at http://www.hach.com/fmmimghach?/CODE%3AIRONFER_AVPP_OTHER_P1873%7C1 and http://www.hach.com/fmmimghach?/CODE%3ASULFIDE_NONE_OTHER_M1965%7C1, respectively, accessed January 6, 2009. Dissolved carbon dioxide (CO_2) concentrations were measured in the field with Titret-Sodium hydroxide titrant with a pH indicator (manufactured by CHEMetrics, Inc., Calverton, Virginia).

Samples for H_2 in groundwater were collected using the bubble-strip method of Chapelle and others (1997) and concentrations were measured in the field using a reduction gas analyzer (Trace Analytical model E-001). Initial gas samples from each well were collected and analyzed after at least 20 minutes of stripping; subsequent samples were collected and analyzed at about 5-minute intervals until consecutive H_2 concentrations stabilized to within 10 percent, a process that often required one hour or more.

Samples for analysis of nitrate plus nitrite, manganese, sulfate, and chloride concentrations were filtered through a 0.45-μm membrane filter into polyethylene bottles, chilled, and sent to the USGS National Water Quality Laboratory (NWQL) in Lakewood, Colorado. Samples for analysis of manganese were acidified in the field with nitric acid to a pH of less than 2 and then analyzed at NWQL by inductively coupled plasma as described by Fishman (1993). Chloride and sulfate were analyzed using ion chromatography as described by Fishman (1993). Nitrate plus nitrite were analyzed colorimetrically by cadmium reduction and diazotization as described by Fishman (1993). The results for the nitrate plus nitrite analyses are referred to simply as "nitrate" in this report because nitrite was not detected historically at the site (Dinicola and others, 2002).

Samples for DOC analysis were filtered through a 0.45-μm filter, collected in amber glass bottles, acidified in the field with sulfuric acid to a pH of less than 2, chilled to less than 4°C, and shipped to NWQL. DOC concentrations were determined using persulfate oxidation and infrared spectrometry as described by Brenton and Arnett (1993).

Samples for VOC analysis were collected in pre-acidified 40-mL glass vials, placed on ice, and shipped to NWQL for subsequent analysis at TestAmerica (TA) Laboratories, Inc. in Denver, Colorado, using purge and trap capillary-column gas chromatography/mass spectrometry according to USEPA Method SW846 8260B (U.S. Environmental Protection Agency, 1996). Samples for analysis of ethane, ethene, and methane were collected in pre-acidified 40-mL glass vials, placed on ice, and shipped to NWQL for subsequent analysis at TA Laboratories, using gas chromatography with a flame-ionization detector according to USEPA Method RSK SOP-175 (U.S. Environmental Protection Agency, 1994). The reporting limit for a given compound often differed between wells because of different degrees of sample dilution by TA Laboratories. The VOC and dissolved gas samples were collected in pre-acidified vials supplied by TA Laboratories; consequently, the vials could not be overfilled during sampling as is recommended in applicable USGS procedures (U.S. Geological Survey, variously dated) to avoid aeration of the sample.

Quality control of geochemical and contaminant sampling for 2007 included the collection of one duplicate sample for selected redox-sensitive analytes and one duplicate sample for VOCs, and for 2008 quality control included the collection of two duplicate samples for redox-sensitive analytes and one duplicate sample for VOCs. A field blank for redox-sensitive analytes and VOCs was collected in 2007 and a field blank was collected for VOCs and organic carbon in 2008. No substantial quality issues were identified in those samples (appendix A).

Natural Attenuation Monitoring Data

The groundwater chemistry data are grouped with regard to location and aquifer of the well or piezometer. Upgradient sites are the two upper aquifer wells (MW1-3 and MW1-20) east of the landfill and one intermediate aquifer well (MW1-33) south of the landfill. Northern plantation sites are all in the upper aquifer and include four wells (1MW-1, MW1-2, MW1-17, and MW1-41) and four piezometers (P1-1, P1-3, P1-4, and P1-5) in or near the northern phytoremediation plantation; piezometer P1-2 generally is dry during June and has not been sampled. Southern plantation sites also are all in the upper aquifer and include three wells (MW1-4, MW1–5, and MW1-16) and five piezometers (P1-6, P1-7, P1-8, P1-9, and P1-10) in or near the southern phytoremediation plantation. Intermediate aquifer sites include four intermediate aquifer wells (MW1-25, MW1-28, MW1-38, and MW1-39) that are downgradient of the landfill; no intermediate aquifer wells are in the footprint of the former landfill.

Geochemical Data and Predominant Redox Conditions

Geochemical data collected by the USGS from piezometers and selected wells at OU 1 from 1996 to 2008 are shown in table 2 (at back of report). Historical geochemical data for wells not sampled in 2007 or 2008 are not included in table 2, but are available in Dinicola (2006).

The predominant redox conditions for all samples were inferred following guidelines described in detail by Dinicola (2006). Redox conditions generally are considered either aerobic when DO concentrations are about 1 mg/L, or anaerobic when DO concentrations are less than 1 mg/L. Anaerobic redox conditions usually can be further specified (and are named) according to the inorganic compound acting as the predominant electron acceptor in a given part of an aquifer. Common anaerobic redox conditions in groundwater are nitrate reducing, manganese reducing, iron reducing, sulfate reducing, and carbon-dioxide reducing (methanogenic). Nitrate reduction, manganese reduction, and iron reduction commonly are together referred to as mildly reducing conditions, whereas sulfate reduction and methanogenesis commonly are referred to as strongly reducing conditions. That distinction is made because different types of biodegradation processes are favored under mildly and strongly reducing conditions. Determination of redox conditions in contaminated groundwater is not a simple task and no universally accepted procedures are available. Data from many OU-1 groundwater samples indicate multiple redox conditions near the well or piezometer. The following two examples illustrate this point.

The first example is from well MW1-41 during 2007 and 2008 where manganese, iron (II), and all methane concentrations were higher than concentrations in upgradient groundwater and were relatively high in comparison to all samples. Those data suggest either manganese- or iron-reducing or methanogenic redox conditions predominated at the time of sampling. No sulfate and very little sulfide were detected at MW1-41, indicating that the predominant redox condition has moved beyond sulfate reduction to methanogenesis. However, the dissolved H_2 concentration of 0.4 nanomolar (nM) at the well suggests iron-reducing conditions (Dinicola, 2006) at the time of sampling. The sample was assigned methanogenesis as the predominant redox condition. The second example is from well MW1-16 during 2007 and 2008 where manganese, iron (II), sulfide, and methane concentrations were much higher than concentrations in upgradient groundwater and were relatively high in comparison to all samples. The sample was assigned sulfate-reduction as the predominant redox condition largely because sulfide is a short-lived by-product of sulfate reduction when high concentrations of reduced iron (II) are available. Elevated sulfide concentrations indicate recent and localized sulfate reduction. Dissolved H_2 could not be measured at well MW1-16 in 2007 because of poor well yield, and the dissolved H_2 concentration in 2008 was only 0.1 nM, indicating iron-reducing conditions. These two examples clearly illustrate that the assignation of predominant redox conditions has some uncertainty.

For 2007 and 2008, predominant redox conditions in the upgradient wells in the upper aquifer (wells MW1-3 and MW1-20) ranged from aerobic to mildly reducing (nitrate reduction, and manganese and iron reduction). These wells have varied between aerobic and sulfate reducing during the 10 years of monitoring (table 2). Concentrations of DOC have been consistently 2 mg/L or less. Redox conditions in the upgradient well in the intermediate aquifer (well MW1-33) have been consistently aerobic.

For the upper aquifer beneath the northern plantation in 2007 and 2008, the strongly reducing conditions (sulfate reduction and methanogenesis) most favorable for reductive dechlorination of VOCs (Bradley, 2003) were inferred for five of eight upper-aquifer wells and piezometers (MW1-17, MW1-41, P1-1, P1-3, and P1-5). The other upper-aquifer wells and piezometers within the plantation had iron-reducing or unspecified anaerobic conditions. Well MW1-17 is included with the northern plantation sites in table 2, although it is between plantations and is not downgradient from any known major contaminant sources. Methane concentrations ranged from 0.26 mg/L (MW1-2 in 2007) to 14 mg/L (P1-3 and P1-5 in 2008), indicating that methanogenic (strongly reducing) redox conditions are common, but not necessarily predominant. Concentrations of DOC, which reflect the availability of electron donor needed to sustain biodegradation processes, ranged from 6.0 mg/L (MW1-2 in 2007) to 23 mg/L (P1-3 in 2008). Concentrations of dissolved carbon dioxide, a byproduct from microbial oxidation of organic compounds, ranged from 11 mg/L (1MW-1 in 2008) to 350 mg/L (MW1-41 and P1-5 in 2007, and P1-1 in 2008). Wells and piezometers with low chlorinated VOC concentrations (MW1-41, P1-1, P1-3, and P1-5), generally had high DOC, dissolved carbon dioxide, and methane concentrations. Conversely, wells and piezometers with high chlorinated VOC concentrations (1MW-1, MW1-2, and P1-4) had low DOC, dissolved carbon dioxide, and methane concentrations. Together those data are compelling evidence that biodegradation has been and continues to be an important process for decreasing contaminant concentrations in the upper aquifer beneath the northern plantation.

For the upper aquifer beneath the southern plantation in 2007 and 2008, the strongly reducing conditions (sulfate reduction and methanogenesis) most favorable for reductive dechlorination of VOCs (Bradley, 2003) were inferred for four of eight upper-aquifer wells and piezometers (MW1-16, P1-6, P1-8, and P1-10). The other upper-aquifer wells and piezometers in the southern plantation had manganese and (or) iron reducing conditions. Methane concentrations ranged from 0.38 mg/L (P1-6 in 2007) to 7.9 mg/L (P1-8 in 2008), indicating that methanogenic (strongly reducing) redox conditions are common, but not necessarily predominant.

The concentrations commonly were less than concentrations measured at northern plantation wells and piezometers. Concentrations of DOC, which reflect the availability of electron donor needed to sustain biodegradation processes, ranged from 1.4 mg/L (MW1-4 in 2007) to 18 mg/L (MW1-16 in 2007), and also were less than concentrations of DOC measured at northern plantation wells and piezometers. Concentrations of dissolved carbon dioxide ranged from less than 10 mg/L (P1-6, P1-8, and P1-9 in 2008) to 190 mg/L (MW1-16 in 2007), and again were less than concentrations of dissolved dioxide measured at northern plantation wells and piezometers. The generalized pattern of relatively high DOC, dissolved carbon dioxide, and methane concentrations at wells and piezometers with relatively low chlorinated VOC concentrations is not consistent in the upper aquifer beneath the southern plantation, although well MW1-4 is highly contaminated with chlorinated VOCs and has DOC concentrations about as low as the nearby upgradient well MW1-20.

Concentrations of H_2 measured in the upper aquifer generally have been lower than concentrations measured before 2002, and only two upper aquifer wells and piezometers (MW1-17 and P1-5) had concentrations greater than 1 nM in 2007 or 2008. However, methane and sulfide concentrations at most upper aquifer wells and piezometers beneath the landfill have been consistently elevated above levels measured upgradient, so the lower H_2 concentrations do not appear to indicate a trend from strongly to mildly reducing predominant redox conditions. Organic carbon concentrations generally decreased at most wells and piezometers for the first few years after pavement was removed in 1999 to install the phytoremediation plantations. However, that downward trend on organic carbon concentrations has not continued beyond about 2004. Overall, except for the apparent trend toward lower dissolved H_2 concentrations, no widespread changes in groundwater redox conditions were identified that should result in either more or less efficient biodegradation of chlorinated VOCs.

Predominant redox conditions in all intermediate aquifer wells downgradient of the landfill have been consistently anaerobic (table 2). Mildly reducing conditions (iron reduction) were inferred for the intermediate aquifer wells at the downgradient margin of the landfill (wells MW1-25 and MW1-28) for 2007 and 2008. Methane concentrations in these wells ranged from 0.67 to 2.8 mg/L and were about twice as high in MW1-25 compared to MW1-28. Concentrations of DOC in these wells ranged from 6.4 to 7.1 mg/L, and have been consistently greater than concentrations of DOC measured in the upgradient intermediate aquifer well MW1-33 (0.5 in 2007 and 0.4 mg/L in 2008). The mildly reducing conditions are somewhat favorable for reductive dechlorination of VOCs (Bradley, 2003).

Volatile Organic Compounds

Volatile organic carbon and dissolved ethane and ethene data collected by the USGS from piezometers and selected intermediate aquifer wells at OU 1 from June 1999 to June 2008 are shown in table 3 (at back of report). The VOC data include concentrations of a subset of the 64 compounds measured using USEPA Method SW846 8260B (U.S. Environmental Protection Agency, 1996). Chemical concentrations are reported as less than the reporting level for samples in which the analyte was neither identified nor detected at concentrations equal to or greater than the reporting level. Historical VOC data for wells not sampled in 2007 or 2008 and for dates before 1999 are not included in table 3, but are in Dinicola (2006) and U.S. Navy (2008). The total CVOCs calculated for each sample is the sum of chlorinated VOC concentrations that were positively detected; concentrations reported as "less than" values were not included in the total. Complete analytical results for the USGS data for 2007–08 and previous years are available from the USGS NWIS web site http://nwis.waterdata.usgs.gov/wa/nwis/qwdata or Dinicola and others (2002), Dinicola (2003, 2004, 2006), and Dinicola and Huffman (2004, 2006, 2007). Complete analytical results for the complimentary Navy VOC data from 1995 through 2007 is available in U.S. Navy (2008).

Volatile Organic Compound Concentrations Beneath the Phytoremediation Plantations

For the northern plantation in 2007 and 2008, chlorinated VOC concentrations at most piezometers were similar to or slightly less than concentrations of chlorinated VOC measured in previous years. In 2008, chlorinated VOCs were not detected at piezometer P1-5, and the only chlorinated VOC that was positively detected at piezometer P1-1 was *cis*-DCE at an estimated concentration of 0.18 μg/L in P1-1 (VOCs were not analyzed at these piezometers in 2007). At piezometer P1-3, chlorinated VOC concentrations in 2007 and 2008 were at the lowest levels since monitoring began in 1999. Most VOC concentrations at piezometer P1-4 in 2007 and 2008 were similar to VOC concentrations measured in previous years except that VC concentrations increased from 280 μg/L in June 2007 to 750 μg/L in June 2008. Since 1999, total CVOC concentrations at P1-4 have been at least two times greater than CVOC concentrations measured at all other piezometers in the northern plantation, including wells 1MW-1, MW1-2, and MW1-41 that are regularly monitored by the Navy (U.S. Navy, 2008). In 2008, measurements of the sum of concentrations of the reductive dechlorination byproducts ethane and ethene were at the highest levels to date at all northern plantation piezometers except P1-1, where the compounds were not positively detected. Those byproduct concentrations provide evidence of reductive dechlorination of chlorinated VOCs.

For the southern plantation in 2007 and 2008, chlorinated VOC concentrations measured in piezometers were often extremely high and varied widely. At piezometer P1-6, the total chlorinated VOC concentration was exceptionally low in 2007 at 380 μg/L, and was then exceptionally high in 2008 at 20,000 μg/L. At piezometer P1-7 in 2008, total chlorinated VOCs, and the individual compounds TCE, *cis*-DCE, and VC, were at the highest concentrations to date. In contrast, total chlorinated VOC concentrations at piezometers P1-8, P1-9 and P1-10 in 2008 were relatively low compared to 1999–2007 levels. Chlorinated VOC concentrations at wells MW1-4 and MW1-16 in the southern plantation also have been highly variable over time. Since 1999, total CVOC concentrations at P1-7 or P1-9 have been the highest measured at all wells and piezometers in the northern plantation. The magnitude and persistence of dissolved-phase chlorinated VOC concentrations in these piezometers indicate non-aqueous phase chloroethenes beneath the southern plantation. The temporal variability in concentrations likely is a result of variations in precipitation and groundwater levels interacting with the non-aqueous phase liquid. In 2007 and 2008, one or both of the reductive dechlorination byproducts ethane and ethene were detected at all southern plantation wells and piezometers, with an ethene concentration as high as 850 μg/L (P1-7 in 2008). Those byproduct concentrations are evidence that reductive dechlorination of dissolved VOCs is ongoing, although non-aqueous phase liquid chloroethenes are not likely to be substantially affected by biodegradation (Dinicola, 2006).

Volatile Organic Compound Concentrations in the Intermediate Aquifer

In 2007, the reductive dechlorination byproducts ethane and ethene were the only VOC concentrations analyzed in samples from the intermediate aquifer. The sum of concentrations of ethane and ethene were 12.1 and 18 μg/L at wells MW1-25 and MW1-28, respectively, indicating ongoing reductive dechlorination. Farther downgradient in the intermediate aquifer beneath the Highway 308 causeway at wells MW1-38 and MW1-39, ethane and ethene were not detected.

In 2008, total chlorinated VOC concentrations in wells MW1-25, MW1-28, and MW1-39 were consistent with previous years. However, VC concentrations in 2008 at these wells were the highest measured to date: 510 µg/L at MW1-25, 930 µg/L at MW1-28, and 3.0 at MW1-39. Along with elevated VC concentrations, the sum of concentrations of ethane and ethene in 2008 were somewhat higher than concentrations measured to date at wells MW1-25 (24 µg/L) and MW1-28 (34 µg/L). These data suggest that either the rate of reductive dechlorination of *cis*-DCE to create VC may have increased, or more non-aqueous phase liquid has dissolved into groundwater.

Summary

Previous investigations report that natural attenuation and biodegradation of chlorinated volatile organic compounds (VOCs) are substantial in groundwater beneath the 9-acre former landfill at Operable Unit 1 (OU 1), Naval Undersea Warfare Center, Division Keyport, Washington. Phytoremediation combined with on-going natural attenuation processes was the preferred remedy selected by the Navy, as specified in the Record of Decision for the site, and the Navy planted two hybrid poplar plantations on the landfill in spring 1999 to remove and to control the migration of chlorinated VOCs in shallow groundwater. The U.S. Geological Survey (USGS) has continued to monitor groundwater geochemistry to ensure that conditions remain favorable for contaminant biodegradation as specified in the Record of Decision. This report presents groundwater geochemical and selected VOC data collected at OU 1 by the USGS during June 18–21, 2007 and June 16–18, 2008 in support of long-term monitoring for natural attenuation.

For 2007 and 2008, strongly reducing conditions (sulfate reduction and methanogenesis) most favorable for reductive dechlorination of VOCs were inferred for 9 of 16 upper-aquifer wells and piezometers in the northern and southern phytoremediation plantations. Predominant redox conditions in groundwater from the intermediate aquifer just downgradient from the landfill remained mildly reducing and somewhat favorable for reductive dechlorination of VOCs. Concentrations of hydrogen (H_2) measured in the upper aquifer generally have been lower than concentrations measured before 2002. However, widespread and relatively high methane and sulfide concentrations suggest that the lower H_2 concentrations measured do not support a trend from strongly to mildly reducing redox conditions because no widespread changes in groundwater redox conditions were identified that should result in less favorable conditions for the reductive dechlorination of the chlorinated VOCs.

For the upper aquifer beneath the northern phytoremediation plantation, chlorinated VOC concentrations in 2007 and 2008 at most piezometers were similar to or slightly less than chlorinated VOC concentrations measured in previous years. The only chlorinated VOC positively detected at piezometers P1-1 and P1-5 was *cis*-DCE; most chlorinated VOC concentrations at piezometer P1-3 were at the lowest levels since monitoring began in 1999. Most VOC concentrations at piezometer P1-4 were similar to VOC concentrations measured in previous years except that vinyl chloride (VC) concentrations inexplicably increased from 280 micrograms per liter (µg/L) in June 2007 to 750 µg/L in June 2008. In 2008, the sum of concentrations of the reductive dechlorination byproducts ethane and ethene were measured at the highest levels to date at most northern plantation wells and piezometers, which is evidence of reductive dechlorination of chlorinated VOCs.

For the upper aquifer beneath the southern phytoremediation plantation, chlorinated VOC concentrations in 2007 and 2008 at the piezometers were most often extremely high and they continued to vary widely over space and time. At piezometer P1-6, the total chlorinated VOC concentration increased from 380 µg/L in 2007 to more than 20,000 µg/L in 2008. At piezometer P1-7 in 2008, trichloroethene, *cis*-1,2-dichloroethene (*cis*-DCE), and VC were measured at the highest concentrations to date, but total chlorinated VOC concentrations at piezometers P1-8, P1-9 and P1-10 in 2008 were relatively low compared to historical levels. The magnitude and persistence of chlorinated VOC concentrations indicate that non-aqueous phase liquid chloroethenes likely are beneath the southern plantation, and the temporal variability in concentrations likely is a result of variations in precipitation and groundwater levels interacting with the non-aqueous phase liquid. The reductive dechlorination byproducts ethane and ethene were detected at all southern plantation wells and piezometers, which is reliable evidence of reductive dechlorination of dissolved VOCs.

For the intermediate aquifer, total chlorinated VOC concentrations in 2008 at wells MW1-25, MW1-28, and MW1-39 were consistent with previous years. However, VC concentrations in 2008 at these wells were the highest measured to date, as were the sum of concentrations of ethane and ethene measured at wells MW1-25 and MW1-28. These data suggest that either the rate of reductive dechlorination of *cis*-DCE to create VC may have increased, or more non-aqueous phase liquid has dissolved into groundwater.

Acknowledgments

The authors thank Douglas Thelin of the Naval Facilities Engineering Command Northwest for his guidance and funding for the continued monitoring. Gene Ellis of the Naval Undersea Warfare Center, Division Keyport, Washington, provided logistical support for field activities. U.S. Geological Survey Washington, Water Science Center staff Stephen Cox, Greg Justin, and Karen Payne assisted with data collection and analysis.

References Cited

American Public Health Association, 1980, Standard methods for the examination of water and wastewater (15th ed.): Washington, D.C., American Public Health Association.

Bradley, P.M., 2003, History and ecology of chloroethene degradation—A review: Bioremediation Journal, v. 7, no. 2, p. 81–109.

Bradley, P.M, Landmeyer, J.E., and Dinicola, R.S., 1998, Anaerobic oxidation of [1,2-14C] dichloroethene under Mn(IV)-reducing conditions: Applied and Environmental Microbiology, v. 64, no. 4, p. 1560–1562.

Brenton, R.W., and Arnett, T.L., 1993, Methods of analysis by the U.S. Geological Survey National Water Quality Laboratory—Determination of dissolved organic carbon by UV-promoted persulfate oxidation and infrared spectrometry: U.S. Geological Survey Open-File Report 92-480, 12 p.

Chapelle, F.H., Vroblesky, D.A., Woodward, J.C., and Lovely, D.R., 1997, Practical considerations for measuring hydrogen concentrations in ground water: Environmental Science and Technology, v. 31, no. 10, p. 2873–2877.

Dinicola, R.S., 2003, Natural attenuation monitoring data during June 2001, Operable Unit 1, Naval Undersea Warfare Center, Division Keyport, Washington: U.S. Geological Survey Open-File Report 03-344, 17 p.

Dinicola, R.S., 2004, Selected natural attenuation monitoring data, Operable Unit 1, Naval Undersea Warfare Center, Division Keyport, Washington: U.S. Geological Survey Open-File Report 2004-1203, 19 p.

Dinicola, R.S., 2006, Continued biodegradation of chloroethene compounds in ground water at Operable Unit 1, Naval Undersea Warfare Center, Division Keyport, Washington: U.S. Geological Survey Scientific Investigations Report 2006-5056, 42 p.

Dinicola, R.S., Cox, S.E., Landmeyer, J.E., and Bradley, P.M., 2002, Natural attenuation of chlorinated volatile organic compounds in ground water at Operable Unit 1, Naval Undersea Weapons Center, Division Keyport, Washington: U.S. Geological Survey Water-Resources Investigations Report 02-4119, 19 p.

Dinicola, R.S., and Huffman, R.L., 2004, Selected natural attenuation monitoring data, Operable Unit 1, Naval Undersea Warfare Center, Division Keyport, Washington, June 2003: U.S. Geological Survey Open-File Report 2004-1330, 19 p.

Dinicola, R.S., and Huffman, R.L., 2006, Selected natural attenuation monitoring data, Operable Unit 1, Naval Undersea Warfare Center, Division Keyport, Washington, June 2005: U.S. Geological Survey Open-File Report 2006-1374, 27 p.

Dinicola, R.S., and Huffman, R.L., 2007, Selected natural attenuation monitoring data, Operable Unit 1, Naval Undersea Warfare Center, Division Keyport, Washington, June 2006: U.S. Geological Survey Open-File Report 2007-1430, 30 p.

Fishman, M.J., ed., 1993, Methods of analysis by the U.S. Geological Survey National Water Quality Laboratory—Determination of inorganic and organic constituents in water and fluvial sediments: U.S. Geological Survey Open-File Report 93-125, 217 p.

Hach Company, 1998, DR/2010 Spectrophotometer Procedures Manual: Loveland, Colo., Hach Company.

URS Consultants, Inc., 1997, Final summary data assessment report for Operable Unit 1, Naval Undersea Warfare Center, Division Keyport, Washington: Seattle, Wash., URS Consultants for Engineering Field Activity, Northwest, Naval Facilities Engineering Command, Poulsbo, Wash., 3 Volumes.

URS Consultants, Inc., 1998, Final record of decision for Operable Unit 1, Naval Undersea Warfare Center, Division Keyport, Washington: Seattle, Wash., URS Consultants, for Engineering Field Activity, Northwest, Naval Facilities Engineering Command, Poulsbo, Wash., 111 p.

URS Greiner, Inc., 1999, Phytoremediation closure report for Operable Unit 1, Naval Undersea Warfare Center, Division Keyport, Washington: Seattle, Wash., URS Greiner, Inc. for Engineering Field Activity, Northwest, Naval Facilities Engineering Command, Poulsbo, Wash.

U.S. Environmental Protection Agency, 1983, Methods for chemical analysis of water and wastes—Office of Research chemical analysis of water and wastes: Washington, D.C., Office of Research and Development Report EPA 600/4-79-020, 552 p.

U.S. Environmental Protection Agency, 1994, RSKSOP 175 rev. no. 2, Sample preparations and calculations for dissolved gas analysis in water samples using a GC headspace equilibration technique: U.S. Environmental Protection Agency Test Methods, Region 1, 14 p., accessed October 2007, at http://www.epa.gov/region1/info/testmethods/pdfs/RSKsop175v2.pdf

U.S. Environmental Protection Agency, 1996, VOCs by GC/MS Capillary column technique, SW-846: Chap. 4.3.2: U.S. Environmental Protection Agency Test Methods, 16 p., accessed October 2007, at http://www.epa.gov/epaoswer/hazwaste/test/pdfs/chap4.pdf

U.S. Geological Survey, variously dated, National field manual for the collection of water-quality data: U.S. Geological Survey Techniques of Water-Resources Investigations, book 9, chaps. A1–A9, accessed August 5, 2009, at http://pubs.water.usgs.gov/twri9A

U.S. Navy, 2008, Final annual report, 2007, Operable Unit 1, Naval Base Kitsap Keyport, Washington: Contract No. N44255-05-D-5101, LTM/O/Task Order 33.

Table 2. Predominant redox conditions at wells and piezometers, and groundwater geochemical data collected at Operable Unit 1, Naval Undersea Warfare Center, Division Keyport, Washington, 1996 to 2008.

[All other data were published in Dinicola and others (2002), Dinicola (2003), and Dinicola (2004); prior to 2000, bicarbonate was calculated from an unfiltered sample. Reported concentrations less than the detection limit usually are estimated. A range of dissolved hydrogen concentrations are shown when equilibration at a single value was never achieved. **Predominant redox conditions:** A, aerobic; An, anaerobic, but specific redox condition could not be determined; Fe, iron reducing; M, methanogenic; Mn, manganese reducing; N, nitrate reducing; S, sulfate reducing. **Abbreviations:** nM, nanomolar; mg/L, milligram per liter; µS/cm, microsiemens per centimeter at 25 degrees Celsius; ORP, oxidation-reduction potential; mV, millivolt. **Symbols:** E, estimated value; R, data rejected (selected 1996 dissolved-oxygen data were rejected because of inadequate well purging; selected 2002 dissolved-hydrogen data were rejected because of interference from downhole instruments); <, actual value is less than value shown; >, actual value is greater than value shown; –, not analyzed]

Well or piezometer No.	Date sampled	Predominant redox condition	Dissolved hydrogen (nM)	Dissolved oxygen (mg/L)	Unfiltered (total) organic carbon (mg/L)	Filtered (dissolved) organic carbon (mg/L)	Filtered nitrate + nitrite (mg/L as N)	Filtered manganese (mg/L)	Filtered iron (II) (mg/L)	Filtered sulfate (mg/L)
					Upgradient					
MW1–3	06-09-99	Fe	0.8	0.4	–	–	–	0.07	<0.01	–
	06-20-00	Fe	.2	.3	2.0	–	0.99	.08	<.01	13
	06-12-01	A	–	4.0	2.3	1.1	1.1	.04	.02	14
	06-10-02	S	2.7	.4	–	1.4	1.6	.10	.01	11
	06-17-03	A	–	4.3	–	1.7	1.8	.09	.05	12
	06-15-04	Mn/Fe	.2	.2	–	1.6	–	.09	<.01	12
	06-20-05	Mn/Fe	<.1	.1	–	1.4	1.6	.10	.01	15
	06-12-06	Mn/Fe	<.1	.1	–	1.4	1.6	.11	<.01	14
	06-18-07	N	–	.6	–	1.8	1.1	.09	<.01	16
	06-16-08	N	–	.6	–	2.0	1.1	.10	<.01	18
MW1–20	06-08-99	Fe	0.9	0.3	–	–	–	0.35	0.03	–
	06-21-00	Fe	.4	<.1	2.2	–	<0.05	.24	.11	16
	06-13-01	S	2.1	.2	3.0	1.4	<.05	.28	.01	20
	06-12-02	An	>100R	.1	–	1.4	<.05	.16	.01	17
	06-17-03	Fe	.5	.2	–	1.7	<.06	.24	.05	18
	06-15-04	Mn/Fe	.1	.9	–	1.6	–	.23	.03	18
	06-20-05	Mn/Fe	.1	.4	–	1.5	<.06	.25	.21	16
	06-13-06	Mn/Fe	.1	.1	–	1.7	<.06	.21	.08	16
	06-18-07	Mn/Fe	–	.2	–	1.8	<.06	.21	.34	14
	06-18-08	A	–	3.4	–	1.5	<.04	.19	.06	19
MW1–33	10-07-98	A	–	3.3	0.1	–	–	0.003	<0.01	–
	06-21-00	A	–	3.8	.7	–	1.3	<.0002	<.01	7.5
	06-11-01	A	–	3.8	1.5	1.4	1.1	<.0003	<.01	8.2
	06-10-02	A	–	3.4	–	1.2	1.1	<.0002	<.01	7.3
	06-17-03	A	–	3.0	–	.7	.98	<.0004	<.01	7.4
	06-15-04	A	–	–	–	.6	–	<.0008	<.01	6.6
	06-20-05	A	–	3.5	–	.5	1.7	<.0006	<.01	6.3
	06-12-06	A	–	3.9	–	.4	1.8	<.0006	.02	5.7
	06-18-07	A	–	4.1	–	.5	1.64	E.0002	–	5.3
	06-16-08	A	–	4.0	–	.4	1.62	<.0004	.03	5.2
					Northern plantation					
1MW-1	09-17-96	Fe	0.4	2.8R	7.0	–	<0.02	0.18	0.24	7.5
	04-16-97	Fe	.8	.4	–	–	.11	–	8.0	1.4
	03-05-98	Fe/S	.2	.1	8.3	–	–	.39	12	–
	10-09-98	Fe	.2	.5	–	–	–	.08	.39	–
	06-21-00	Mn/Fe	.1	.5	12	–	<.05	.96	13	.9
	06-11-01	Fe	.6	.7	13	12	<.05	.24	2.9	2.2
	06-10-02	Fe	.4	.2	–	14	<.05	.37	7.3	1.7
	06-17-03	Fe	.1	.1	–	10	<.06	.17	1.2	2.2
	06-16-04	Fe	.2	.1	–	7.7	–	.09	.38	2.0
	06-21-05	Fe	.1	.1	–	9.5	<.06	.12	1.8	1.7
	06-12-06	Mn/Fe	<.1	.2	–	8.5	<.06	.12	.8	1.9
	06-19-07	An	.3	.1	–	6.8	E.05	1.3	.72	6.4
	06-17-08	An	.2	.2	–	9.6	<.04	.13	1.4	1.3

Table 2. Predominant redox conditions at wells and piezometers, and groundwater geochemical data collected at Operable Unit 1, Naval Undersea Warfare Center, Division Keyport, Washington, 1996 to 2008.—Continued

[All other data were published in Dinicola and others (2002), Dinicola (2003), and Dinicola (2004); prior to 2000, bicarbonate was calculated from an unfiltered sample. Reported concentrations less than the detection limit usually are estimated. A range of dissolved hydrogen concentrations are shown when equilibration at a single value was never achieved. **Predominant redox conditions:** A, aerobic; An, anaerobic, but specific redox condition could not be determined; Fe, iron reducing; M, methanogenic; Mn, manganese reducing; N, nitrate reducing; S, sulfate reducing. **Abbreviations:** nM, nanomolar; mg/L, milligram per liter; µS/cm, microsiemens per centimeter at 25 degrees Celsius; ORP, oxidation-reduction potential; mV, millivolt. **Symbols**: E, estimated value; R, data rejected (selected 1996 dissolved-oxygen data were rejected because of inadequate well purging; selected 2002 dissolved-hydrogen data were rejected because of interference from downhole instruments); <, actual value is less than value shown; >, actual value is greater than value shown; –, not analyzed]

Well or piezometer No.	Date sampled	Predominant redox condition	Unfiltered sulfide (mg/L)	Dissolved methane (mg/L)	Dissolved carbon dioxide (mg/L)	Filtered bicarbonate (mg/L)	pH (units)	Specific conductance (µS/cm)	ORP (mV)	Filtered chloride (mg/L)
				Upgradient						
MW1-3	06-09-99	Fe	<0.01	–	–	81	6.0	202	–	–
	06-20-00	Fe	<.01	0.02	–	82	5.9	205	180	8.4
	06-12-01	A	<.01	.12	–	90	6.1	203	220	10
	06-10-02	S	<.01	.06	140	80	5.8	182	400	9.7
	06-17-03	A	–	.02	80	–	6.0	199	200	10
	06-15-04	Mn/Fe	<.01	.01	–	73	5.7	205	195	9.1
	06-20-05	Mn/Fe	<.01	–	<50	–	6.0	192	–	7.5
	06-12-06	Mn/Fe	<.01	.004	40	–	5.5	243	136	7.0
	06-18-07	N	.01	–	41	–	5.9	209	–	5.9
	06-16-08	N	<.01	–	80	–	6.0	198	260	5.1
MW1-20	06-08-99	Fe	<0.01	–	–	260	6.7	546	–	–
	06-21-00	Fe	<.01	0.01	–	240	6.8	530	79	14
	06-13-01	S	<.01	.27	–	260	6.4	544	250	33
	06-12-02	An	<.01	.06	97	250	7.0	701	180	29
	06-17-03	Fe	–	.09	90	–	6.3	491	290	32
	06-15-04	Mn/Fe	<.01	.03	–	260	6.4	552	98	35
	06-20-05	Mn/Fe	<.01	–	80	–	6.3	520	87	28
	06-13-06	Mn/Fe	<.01	.03	60	–	6.3	574	70	31
	06-18-07	Mn/Fe	<.01	–	40	–	6.8	508	7.2	25
	06-18-08	A	–	–	70	–	6.6	517	74	38
MW1-33	10-07-98	A	<0.01	–	–	78	6.6	177	–	–
	06-21-00	A	<.01	0.05	–	74	6.7	164	160	4.0
	06-11-01	A	<.01	.07	–	71	6.2	154	300	3.6
	06-10-02	A	<.01	.004	31	81	6.5	138	360	3.4
	06-17-03	A	<.01	.01	25	–	6.3	156	110	3.7
	06-15-04	A	–	<.005	13	–	6.7	165	–	4.0
	06-20-05	A	–	–	18	–	6.6	154	–	4.1
	06-12-06	A	–	.002	18	–	6.7	159	72	4.3
	06-18-07	A	–	–	12	–	6.3	157	–	4.3
	06-18-08	A	–	–	13	–	6.7	153	157	4.3
				Northern plantation						
1MW-1	09-17-96	Fe	<0.01	10	–	640	7.9	–	–	43
	04-16-97	Fe	.01	29	–	1,100	7.2	–	–	–
	03-05-98	Fe/S	.06	–	–	–	–	–	–	–
	10-09-98	Fe	.01	–	–	660	7.7	1,080	–	–
	06-21-00	Mn/Fe	<.01	.39	–	590	7.0	1,070	-92	44
	06-11-01	Fe	<.01	5.6	–	550	7.1	974	-110	50
	06-10-02	Fe	<.01	14	77	520	7.7	835	-160	54
	06-17-03	Fe	<.01	7.1	50	–	7.3	847	–	54
	06-16-04	Fe	.03	1.8	18	–	7.0	843	-184	57
	06-21-05	Fe	.02	–	20	–	7.1	827	-108	48
	06-12-06	Mn/Fe	.01	3.4	10	–	7.4	787	-134	48
	06-19-07	An	.04	1.7	18	–	7.3	753	-164	7.7
	06-17-08	An	.01	5.4	11	–	7.4	737		40

Table 2. Predominant redox conditions at wells and piezometers, and groundwater geochemical data collected at Operable Unit 1, Naval Undersea Warfare Center, Division Keyport, Washington, 1996 to 2008.—Continued

[All other data were published in Dinicola and others (2002), Dinicola (2003), and Dinicola (2004); prior to 2000, bicarbonate was calculated from an unfiltered sample. Reported concentrations less than the detection limit usually are estimated. A range of dissolved hydrogen concentrations are shown when equilibration at a single value was never achieved. **Predominant redox conditions:** A, aerobic; An, anaerobic, but specific redox condition could not be determined; Fe, iron reducing; M, methanogenic; Mn, manganese reducing; N, nitrate reducing; S, sulfate reducing. **Abbreviations:** nM, nanomolar; mg/L, milligram per liter; µS/cm, microsiemens per centimeter at 25 degrees Celsius; ORP, oxidation-reduction potential; mV, millivolt. **Symbols:** E, estimated value; R, data rejected (selected 1996 dissolved-oxygen data were rejected because of inadequate well purging; selected 2002 dissolved-hydrogen data were rejected because of interference from downhole instruments); <, actual value is less than value shown; >, actual value is greater than value shown; –, not analyzed]

Well or piezometer No.	Date sampled	Predominant redox condition	Dissolved hydrogen (nM)	Dissolved oxygen (mg/L)	Unfiltered (total) organic carbon (mg/L)	Filtered (dissolved) organic carbon (mg/L)	Filtered nitrate + nitrite (mg/L as N)	Filtered manganese (mg/L)	Filtered iron (II) (mg/L)	Filtered sulfate (mg/L)
					Northern plantation—Continued					
MW1–2	09-17-96	A	0.5	2.4R	6.0	–	<0.02	0.05	0.23	4.6
	04-16-97	Fe	.7	.2	–	–	<.02	–	.13	4.6
	03-02-98	Fe	.3	–	–	–	–	–	.16	–
	10-07-98	Fe	.1	.1	–	–	–	.05	.14	–
	06-09-99	Fe	.9	.2	–	–	–	.08	.09	–
	06-21-00	Fe	.3	.1	6.0	–	<.05	.06	.10	4.3
	06-12-01	S	3.5	.3	5.3	5.0	<.05	.08	.29	5.4
	06-11-02	An	>20R	.1	–	45	<.05	.09	.27	4.2
	06-18-03	Fe	.2	.1	–	6.0	<.06	.10	.29	4.3
	06-17-04	Fe	.2	.2	–	6.7	–	.10	1.0	4.3
	06-22-05	Fe	<.1	<1	–	20	<.06	.10	.44	4.4
	06-12-06	Fe	.1	.1	–	5.9	<.06	.10	.76	3.7
	06-19-07	Fe	.2	<1	–	6.0	<.06	.11	.84	3.8
	06-17-08	Fe	<.1	1	–	6.3	<.04	.11	.64	3.4
MW1–15	09-16-96	Fe	0.2	<0.1	50	–	<0.02	5.7	68	0.1
	04-16-97	Fe/S	.8	<.1	–	–	<.02	–	77	.1
	03-05-98	S	1.2	<.1	33	–	–	18	51	–
	10-09-98	S	2.9	<.1	–	–	–	5.8	64	–
	06-15-04	S	3.2	.8	–	27	–	63	36	<.2
MW1–17	09-17-96	Fe	.7	<.1	23	–	<.02	1.3	62	4.3
	04-16-97	Fe	.6	<.1	–	–	<.02	–	37	68
	10-09-98	Fe	–	<.1	–	–	–	.80	56	–
	06-22-00	S	1.2	<.1	11	–	–	1.2	68	–
	06-12-01	S	2.0–2.7	.4	9.2	8.0	<.05	1.2	48	12
	06-17-04	S	2.5	<.1	–	7.5	–	.68	>10	18
	06-20-05	S	1.5	<.1	–	6.1	<.06	.43	27	7.8
	06-20-07	S	1.0	<.1	–	8.1	<.06	.40	22	11
	06-18-08	S	1.1	<.1	–	6.1	<.04	.33	17	7.3
MW1–41	06-09-99	S	1.0	0.3	–	–	–	2.2	60	–
	06-21-00	S	1.2	.1	22	–	<0.05	3.5	55	<0.3
	06-11-01	S	2.0	.3	14	14	<.05	3.7	66	30
	06-10-02	S	2.2	.8	–	20	<.05	3.6	52	.4
	06-18-03	S	1.9	<.1	–	19	<.06	3.9	50	<.2
	06-17-04	S	2.2	.1	–	19	–	4.0	57	<.2
	06-20-05	Fe/S	.8	.1	–	17	<.06	3.9	73	<2
	06-12-06	Fe/S	.7	<.1	–	18	<.06	3.8	28	<.2
	06-19-07	M	.4	<1	–	20	<.06	3.8	66	<.18
	06-16-08	M	.4	<1	–	20	<.04	3.4	41	<.18

Table 2   17

Table 2. Predominant redox conditions at wells and piezometers, and groundwater geochemical data collected at Operable Unit 1, Naval Undersea Warfare Center, Division Keyport, Washington, 1996 to 2008.—Continued

[All other data were published in Dinicola and others (2002), Dinicola (2003), and Dinicola (2004); prior to 2000, bicarbonate was calculated from an unfiltered sample. Reported concentrations less than the detection limit usually are estimated. A range of dissolved hydrogen concentrations are shown when equilibration at a single value was never achieved. **Predominant redox conditions:** A, aerobic; An, anaerobic, but specific redox condition could not be determined; Fe, iron reducing; M, methanogenic; Mn, manganese reducing; N, nitrate reducing; S, sulfate reducing. **Abbreviations:** nM, nanomolar; mg/L, milligram per liter; μS/cm, microsiemens per centimeter at 25 degrees Celsius; ORP, oxidation-reduction potential; mV, millivolt. **Symbols:** E, estimated value; R, data rejected (selected 1996 dissolved-oxygen data were rejected because of inadequate well purging; selected 2002 dissolved-hydrogen data were rejected because of interference from downhole instruments); <, actual value is less than value shown; >, actual value is greater than value shown; –, not analyzed]

Well or piezometer No.	Date sampled	Predominant redox condition	Unfiltered sulfide (mg/L)	Dissolved methane (mg/L)	Dissolved carbon dioxide (mg/L)	Filtered bicarbonate (mg/L)	pH (units)	Specific conduc- tance (μS/cm)	ORP (mV)	Filtered chloride (mg/L)
				Northern plantation—Continued						
MW1-2	09-17-96	A	<0.01	1.2	–	510	6.9	–	–	50
	04-16-97	Fe	<.01	2.5	–	1,100	6.7	–	–	–
	03-02-98	Fe	–	–	–	–	–	–	–	–
	10-07-98	Fe	<.01	–	–	300	6.7	868	–	–
	06-09-99	Fe	<.01	–	–	490	6.8	901	–	–
	06-21-00	Fe	<.01	.04	–	460	6.8	870	37	36
	06-12-01	S	<.01	.78	–	470	6.5	853	27	48
	06-11-02	An	<.01	.92	200	500	6.6	829	200	37
	06-18-03	Fe	<.01	.98	160	–	6.4	870	62	41
	06-17-04	Fe	–	.33	50	–	6.6	858	-	40
	06-22-05	Fe	<.01	–	75	–	6.3	720	-14	35
	06-12-06	Fe	<.01	.50	115	–	6.5	815	-47	34
	06-19-07	Fe	<.01	.26	45	–	6.4	820	-50	30
	06-17-08	Fe	<.01	.43	40	–	6.6	797		26
MW1–15	09-16-96	Fe	<0.01	8.8	–	1,200	–	–	–	18
	04-16-97	Fe/S	.03	44	–	1,600	6.3	–	–	-
	03-05-98	S	<.01	–	–	–	–	–	–	–
	10-09-98	S	<.01	–	–	750	6.3	1,110	–	–
	06-15-04	S	<.01	.22	760	–	6.3	1,200	–	16
MW1–17	09-17-96	Fe	<.01	8.9	–	760	6.5	–	–	61
	04-16-97	Fe	.02	23	–	1,200	6.6	–	–	–
	10-09-98	Fe	.02	–	–	510	6.4	1,740	–	–
	06-22-00	S	.02	2.8	–	450	6.5	1,260	-41	160
	06-12-01	S	.01	9.4	–	500	6.5	1,200	-280	120
	06-17-04	S	–	37	70	–	6.5	318	-	150
	06-20-05	S	.04	–	80	–	6.3	563	-144	74
	06-20-07	S	.03	2.9	55	–	6.5	635	-123	96
	06-18-08	S	.04	5.5	26	–	6.6	551	-109	59
MW1–41	06-09-99	S	0.01	–	–	860	6.6	1,260	–	–
	06-21-00	S	<.01	1.9	–	1,000	6.5	1,500	-75	8.3
	06-11-01	S	.02	25	–	980	6.3	1,330	-89	9.9
	06-10-02	S	.04	21	540	830	6.3	1,190	-68	7.9
	06-18-03	S	.03	14	500	–	6.3	1,280	93	9.5
	06-17-04	S	.02	7.4	450	–	6.1	1,300	-165	11
	06-20-05	Fe/S	.01	–	500	–	6.4	1,300	–	8.7
	06-12-06	Fe/S	.02	8.5	310	–	6.3	1,240	-103	8.4
	06-19-07	M	.01	6.3	350	–	6.7	1,280	-124	8.7
	06-16-08	M	.01	9.9	300	–	6.4	1,240	-93	11

Table 2. Predominant redox conditions at wells and piezometers, and ground-water geochemical data collected at Operable Unit 1, Naval Undersea Warfare Center, Division Keyport, Washington, 1996 to 2007.—Continued

[All other data were published in Dinicola and others (2002), Dinicola (2003), and Dinicola (2004); prior to 2000, bicarbonate was calculated from an unfiltered sample. Reported concentrations less than the detection limit usually are estimated. A range of dissolved hydrogen concentrations are shown when equilibration at a single value was never achieved. **Predominant redox conditions:** A, aerobic; An, anaerobic, but specific redox condition could not be determined; Fe, iron reducing; M, methanogenic; Mn, manganese reducing; N, nitrate reducing; S, sulfate reducing. **Abbreviations:** nM, nanomolar; mg/L, milligram per liter; µS/cm, microsiemens per centimeter at 25 degrees Celsius; ORP, oxidation-reduction potential; mV, millivolt. **Symbols:** E, estimated value; R, data rejected (selected 1996 dissolved-oxygen data were rejected because of inadequate well purging; selected 2002 dissolved-hydrogen data were rejected because of interference from downhole instruments); <, actual value is less than value shown; >, actual value is greater than value shown; –, not analyzed]

Well or piezometer No.	Date sampled	Predominant redox condition	Dissolved hydrogen (nM)	Dissolved oxygen (mg/L)	Unfiltered (total) organic carbon (mg/L)	Filtered (dissolved) organic carbon (mg/L)	Filtered nitrate + nitrite (mg/L as N)	Filtered manganese (mg/L)	Filtered iron (II) (mg/L)	Filtered sulfate (mg/L)
					Northern plantation—Continued					
P1–1	06-09-99	Fe	0.7	0.4	–	–	–	4.0	59	–
	06-11-02	S	1.4	<.1	–	17	<0.05	2.7	40	<0.1
	06-18-03	S	1.5	<.1	–	18	<.06	3.4	32	<.2
	06-17-04	S	1.9	.1	–	16	–	3.1	39	<.2
	06-22-05	Fe/S	.6	<.1	–	15	<.06	3.1	68	<.2
	06-12-06	Fe/S	.3	<.1	–	16	<.06	2.9	54	<.2
	06-19-07	S/M	.3	<.1	–	15	<.06	2.0	49	<.18
	06-16-08	S/M	.6	.1	–	14	<.04	2.1	32	<.18
P1–3	06-09-99	Fe	0.4	0.2	–	–	–	1.0	19	–
	06-11-02	Fe	.3	<.1	–	45	<0.05	2.6	39	1.0
	06-18-03	Fe	.3	.1	–	19	<.06	2.0	29	1.8
	06-17-04	Fe	.7	<.1	–	21	–	2.8	>10	.55
	06-22-05	Fe	.2	<.1	–	20	<.06	2.8	60	.38
	06-12-06	Fe	.2	<.1	–	20	<.06	2.5	39	.2
	06-19-07	Fe/S	.3	<.1	–	22	<.06	2.5	40	.24
	06-17-08	S/M	.9	<.1	–	23	<.04	2.9	32	<.18
P1–4	06-09-99	Fe	0.7	0.3	–	–	–	0.34	2.6	–
	06-13-01	Fe	.1	.5	9.8	8.7	<0.05	.38	3.4	3.8
	06-11-02	Fe	.2	.1	–	8.0	<.05	2.6	3.7	3.5
	06-18-03	Fe	.2	.1	–	7.0	<.06	.43	4.1	4.0
	06-17-04	Fe	.1	.1	–	7.6	–	.42	3.0	4.0
	06-21-05	Fe	.1	.1	–	6.7	<.06	.38	2.3	4.6
	06-12-06	Fe	.1	<.1	–	6.8	<.06	.35	1.8	4.3
	06-19-07	Fe	.3	<.1	–	7.1	<.06	.35	3.2	4.7
	06-16-08	Fe	<.1	<.1	–	7.7	<.04	.35	3.5	4.4
P1–5	06-08-99	S	3.0	0.3	–	–	–	3.1	72	–
	06-10-02	S	1.7	.1	–	25	<0.05	2.6	62	<0.6
	06-18-03	S	2.2	.1	–	24	<.06	3.1	54	<.2
	06-17-04	S	2.1	<.1	–	23	–	3.1	>10	<.2
	06-21-05	Fe/S	.8	.1	–	22	<.06	3.5	74	E.1
	06-12-06	Fe/S	.8	<.1	–	21	<.06	3.6	66	E.1
	06-19-07	S/M	.3	<.1	–	22	<.06	3.2	48	<.2
	06-16-08	S/M	1.0	M	–	21	<.04	3.6	44	<.2

Table 2   19

Table 2. Predominant redox conditions at wells and piezometers, and groundwater geochemical data collected at Operable Unit 1, Naval Undersea Warfare Center, Division Keyport, Washington, 1996 to 2008.—Continued

[All other data were published in Dinicola and others (2002), Dinicola (2003), and Dinicola (2004); prior to 2000, bicarbonate was calculated from an unfiltered sample. Reported concentrations less than the detection limit usually are estimated. A range of dissolved hydrogen concentrations are shown when equilibration at a single value was never achieved. **Predominant redox conditions:** A, aerobic; An, anaerobic, but specific redox condition could not be determined; Fe, iron reducing; M, methanogenic; Mn, manganese reducing; N, nitrate reducing; S, sulfate reducing. **Abbreviations:** nM, nanomolar; mg/L, milligram per liter; μS/cm, microsiemens per centimeter at 25 degrees Celsius; ORP, oxidation-reduction potential; mV, millivolt. **Symbols:** E, estimated value; R, data rejected (selected 1996 dissolved-oxygen data were rejected because of inadequate well purging; selected 2002 dissolved-hydrogen data were rejected because of interference from downhole instruments); <, actual value is less than value shown; >, actual value is greater than value shown; –, not analyzed]

Well or piezometer No.	Date sampled	Predominant redox condition	Unfiltered sulfide (mg/L)	Dissolved methane (mg/L)	Dissolved carbon dioxide (mg/L)	Filtered bicarbonate (mg/L)	pH (units)	Specific conduc- tance (μS/cm)	ORP (mV)	Filtered chloride (mg/L)
				Northern plantation—Continued						
P1–1	06-09-99	Fe	<0.01	–	–	930	6.4	1,350	–	–
	06-11-02	S	<.01	29	400	650	6.3	987	-80	9.3
	06-18-03	S	.02		450	–	6.2	1,030	78	11
	06-17-04	S	.02	3.7	430	–	6.0	987	-153	9.2
	06-22-05	Fe	<.01	10	370	–	6.3	847	-72	7.1
	06-12-06	Fe/S	.01	7.8	225	–	6.2	979	-108	7.2
	06-19-07	S/M	.02	8.1	160	–	6.1	920	-139	5.7
	06-16-08	S/M	.02	12	350	–	6.5	914	-76	4.4
P1–3	06-09-99	Fe	0.04	–	–	730	6.8	1,470	–	–
	06-11-02	Fe	.03	24	400	820	6.4	1,340	-73	61
	06-18-03	Fe	.03	–	350	–	6.4	1,400	73	90
	06-17-04	Fe	<.01	5.7	330	–	6.5	1,350	–	57
	06-22-05	Fe	.03	8.4	320	–	6.4	1,200	-88	68
	06-12-06	Fe	.03	7.1	330	–	6	1,440	-152	51
	06-19-07	Fe/S	.03	7.1	260	–	6.5	1,420	-136	55
	06-17-08	S/M	.03	14	200	–	6.4	1,230		31
P1–4	06-09-99	Fe	0.02	–	–	450	6.9	867	–	–
	06-13-01	Fe	<.01	0.93	–	390	6.6	761	-78	53
	06-11-02	Fe	<.01	5.9	90	380	6.7	734	-86	56
	06-18-03	Fe	.01	4.2	70	–	6.6	778	65	59
	06-17-04	Fe	.02	1.8	60	–	6.4	782	-163	48
	06-21-05	Fe	<.01	1.8	42	–	6.6	750	-83	47
	06-12-06	Fe	<.01	1.7	32	–	6.4	823	-94	44
	06-19-07	Fe	<.01	2.5	26	–	6.7	745	-99	44
	06-16-08	Fe	.01	3.1	20	–	6.9	749	-86	40
P1–5	06-08-99	S	0.01	–	–	850	6.2	1,320	–	–
	06-10-02	S	.02	23	400	730	6.2	1,200	-59	17
	06-18-03	S	.02	18	650	–	6.2	1,150	65	16
	06-17-04	S	–	5.8	450	–	6.4	1,160	-	14
	06-21-05	Fe/S	.04	9.4	400	–	6.3	1,150	-65	13
	06-12-06	Fe/S	.05	6.8	370	–	5.8	1,100	-106	9.9
	06-19-07	S/M	.04	8.5	350	–	6.3	1,030	-104	9.3
	06-16-08	S/M	.04	14	275	–	6.3	1,080	29	10

Table 2.   Predominant redox conditions at wells and piezometers, and groundwater geochemical data collected at Operable Unit 1, Naval Undersea Warfare Center, Division Keyport, Washington, 1996 to 2008.—Continued

[All other data were published in Dinicola and others (2002), Dinicola (2003), and Dinicola (2004); prior to 2000, bicarbonate was calculated from an unfiltered sample. Reported concentrations less than the detection limit usually are estimated. A range of dissolved hydrogen concentrations are shown when equilibration at a single value was never achieved. **Predominant redox conditions:** A, aerobic; An, anaerobic, but specific redox condition could not be determined; Fe, iron reducing; M, methanogenic; Mn, manganese reducing; N, nitrate reducing; S, sulfate reducing. **Abbreviations:** nM, nanomolar; mg/L, milligram per liter; μS/cm, microsiemens per centimeter at 25 degrees Celsius; ORP, oxidation-reduction potential; mV, millivolt. **Symbols:** E, estimated value; R, data rejected (selected 1996 dissolved-oxygen data were rejected because of inadequate well purging; selected 2002 dissolved-hydrogen data were rejected because of interference from downhole instruments); <, actual value is less than value shown; >, actual value is greater than value shown; –, not analyzed]

Well or piezometer No.	Date sampled	Predominant redox condition	Dissolved hydrogen (nM)	Dissolved oxygen (mg/L)	Unfiltered (total) organic carbon (mg/L)	Filtered (dissolved) organic carbon (mg/L)	Filtered nitrate + nitrite (mg/L as N)	Filtered manganese (mg/L)	Filtered iron (II) (mg/L)	Filtered sulfate (mg/L)
					Southern plantation					
MW1–4	09-17-96	Fe	0.5	2.8R	2.0	–	<0.02	0.28	1.8	7.1
	04-16-97	Fe	.6	.4	–	–	.24	–	<.01	8.6
	03-03-98	S	1.7	.2	4.0	–	–	.10	.01	–
	10-08-98	Fe	.2	.5	–	–	–	–	.28	–
	06-07-99	Fe	.9	.1	–	–	–	.20	1.2	–
	06-22-00	Fe	.2	.1	8.6	–	–	.70	–	5.5
	06-14-01	S	0 9–3.2	.5	2.9	2.5	.08	.54	1.6	5.4
	06-13-02	S	2.4	.1	–	3.8	.08	.47	1.2	5.5
	06-20-03	Fe	.8	.1	–	2.5	<.06	.53	.22	5.7
	06-18-04	Fe	.2	.1	–	2.7	–	.61	.12	5.9
	06-23-05	Mn/Fe	.3	.1	–	.7	<.06	.14	.03	8.8
	06-13-06	Mn/Fe	<.1	.1	–	3.9	<.06	.79	.19	5.7
	06-20-07	Mn/Fe	.1	<.1	–	1.4	<.06	.29	.23	7.5
	06-18-08	Mn/Fe	<.1	.1	–	2.6	E.03	.42	.19	7.1
MW1–5	09-17-96	S	1.2	<0.1	15	–	<0.02	1.6	19	6.4
	04-16-97	Fe	.5	<.1	–	–	.08	–	3.1	2.8
	03-04-98	Fe	.7	<.1	12	–	–	1.3	4.5	–
	10-08-98	S	2.4	<.1	–	–	–	1.5	11	–
	06-08-99	Fe	.6	.3	–	–	–	1.2	31	–
	06-22-00	Fe	–	<.1	17	–	–	1.5	39	6.4
	06-13-01	Fe	.8	.3	10	9.6	.12	1.5	25	6.0
	06-13-02	S	3.4	.5	–	11	.14	1.5	20	6.3
	06-20-03	Fe	.1	.1	–	11	<.06	1.5	30	6.8
	06-18-04	Fe	.1	.4	–	7 2	–	1.8	>10	5.6
	06-22-05	Fe	<.1	<.1	–	8 2	.16	1.2	27	6.7
	06-13-06	Fe	<.1	.1	–	7.8	.08	1.3	14	6.0
	06-20-07	Fe	.1	<.1	–	8.0	<.06	.10	21	1.7
	06-18-08	Fe	<.1	0.3	–	5.9	.15	1.0	16	7.3

Table 2   21

Table 2. Predominant redox conditions at wells and piezometers, and groundwater geochemical data collected at Operable Unit 1, Naval Undersea Warfare Center, Division Keyport, Washington, 1996 to 2008.—Continued

[All other data were published in Dinicola and others (2002), Dinicola (2003), and Dinicola (2004); prior to 2000, bicarbonate was calculated from an unfiltered sample. Reported concentrations less than the detection limit usually are estimated. A range of dissolved hydrogen concentrations are shown when equilibration at a single value was never achieved. **Predominant redox conditions:** A, aerobic; An, anaerobic, but specific redox condition could not be determined; Fe, iron reducing; M, methanogenic; Mn, manganese reducing; N, nitrate reducing; S, sulfate reducing. **Abbreviations:** nM, nanomolar; mg/L, milligram per liter; µS/cm, microsiemens per centimeter at 25 degrees Celsius; ORP, oxidation-reduction potential; mV, millivolt. **Symbols**: E, estimated value; R, data rejected (selected 1996 dissolved-oxygen data were rejected because of inadequate well purging; selected 2002 dissolved-hydrogen data were rejected because of interference from downhole instruments); <, actual value is less than value shown; >, actual value is greater than value shown; –, not analyzed]

Well or piezometer No.	Date sampled	Predominant redox condition	Unfiltered sulfide (mg/L)	Dissolved methane (mg/L)	Dissolved carbon dioxide (mg/L)	Filtered bicarbonate (mg/L)	pH (units)	Specific conductance (µS/cm)	ORP (mV)	Filtered chloride (mg/L)
				Southern plantation						
MW1–4	09-17-96	Fe	<0.01	1.2	–	130	6.9	–	–	15
	04-16-97	Fe	<.01	.70	–	270	7.3	–	–	–
	03-03-98	S	<.01	–	–	–	–	–	–	–
	10-08-98	Fe	<.01	–	–	170	6.7	368	–	–
	06-07-99	Fe	<.01	–	–	180	6.6	350	–	–
	06-22-00	Fe	<.01	.56	–	230	6.8	412	-26	19
	06-14-01	S	<.01	3.7	–	180	6.5	360	-8	22
	06-13-02	S	<.01	5.2	60	190	6.6	442	-14	20
	06-20-03	Fe	<.01	3.7	40	–	6.7	324	–	17
	06-18-04	Fe	<.01	1.1	50	–	6.0	320	91	23
	06-23-05	Mn	<.01	–	<10	–	7.9	203	45	7 3
	06-13-06	Mn/Fe	.01	2.1	30	–	6.6	362	-1	20
	06-20-07	Mn/Fe	<.01	.53	14	–	7.0	252	-58	11
	06-18-08	Mn/Fe	<.01	1.7	12	–	7.2	279		15
MW1–5	09-17-96	S	<0.01	2.4	–	410	6.7	–	–	21
	04-16–97	Fe	.03	18	–	1,400	6.6	–	–	–
	03-04-98	Fe	<.01	–	–	–	–	–	–	–
	10-08-98	S	<.01	–	–	410	6.4	1,740	–	–
	06-08-99	Fe	.01	–	–	510	6.5	855	–	–
	06-22-00	Fe	<.01	1.1	–	460	6.6	790	-80	19
	06-13-01	Fe	.01	2.4	–	470	6.4	766	-70	12
	06-13-02	S	.02	7.4	180	740	6.5	608	-77	9.6
	06-20-03	Fe	.03	4.9	180	–	6.4	711	–	10
	06-18-04	Fe	–	2.4	200	–	6.5	795	–	9.8
	06-22-05	Fe	.02	-	70	–	6.3	570	-95	9.5
	06-13-06	Fe	.02	1.9	50	–	6.5	603	-85	8.5
	06-20-07	Fe	.03	1.1	100	–	6.5	603	-106	44
	06-18-08	Fe	.01	1.8	100	–	6.6	562	–	8.4

Table 2. Predominant redox conditions at wells and piezometers, and groundwater geochemical data collected at Operable Unit 1, Naval Undersea Warfare Center, Division Keyport, Washington, 1996 to 2008.—Continued

[All other data were published in Dinicola and others (2002), Dinicola (2003), and Dinicola (2004); prior to 2000, bicarbonate was calculated from an unfiltered sample. Reported concentrations less than the detection limit usually are estimated. A range of dissolved hydrogen concentrations are shown when equilibration at a single value was never achieved. **Predominant redox conditions:** A, aerobic; An, anaerobic, but specific redox condition could not be determined; Fe, iron reducing; M, methanogenic; Mn, manganese reducing; N, nitrate reducing; S, sulfate reducing. **Abbreviations:** nM, nanomolar; mg/L, milligram per liter; µS/cm, microsiemens per centimeter at 25 degrees Celsius; ORP, oxidation-reduction potential; mV, millivolt. **Symbols:** E, estimated value; R, data rejected (selected 1996 dissolved-oxygen data were rejected because of inadequate well purging; selected 2002 dissolved-hydrogen data were rejected because of interference from downhole instruments); <, actual value is less than value shown; >, actual value is greater than value shown; –, not analyzed]

Well or piezometer No.	Date sampled	Predominant redox condition	Dissolved hydrogen (nM)	Dissolved oxygen (mg/L)	Unfiltered (total) organic carbon (mg/L)	Filtered (dissolved) organic carbon (mg/L)	Filtered nitrate + nitrite (mg/L as N)	Filtered manganese (mg/L)	Filtered iron (II) (mg/L)	Filtered sulfate (mg/L)
					Southern plantation—Continued					
MW1–16	09-17-96	S	2.1	<0.1	480	–	<0.02	3.9	130	0.2
	04-16-97	Fe/S	.8	<.1	–	–	<.02	–	120	2.2
	03-04-98	Fe	.7	.3	350	–	–	18	100	–
	10-08-98	M	9.6	<.1	–	–	–	5.4	180	–
	06-07-99	M	6.8	.6	–	–	–	>5	140	–
	06-22-00	S	–	.1	61	–	–	1.9	60	1.2
	06-14-01	S	1.7	.2	64	66	.33	2.4	56	1.1
	06-13-02	M	4.6–7.6	.9	–	71	<.05	3.2	38	.4
	06-20-03	S	2.2	.2	–	29	<.6	2.1	37	.6
	06-22-04	–	–	.1	–	36	–	2.1	>10	.1
	06-23-05	Fe/S	.5	.1	–	20	<.06	2.0	66	.4
	06-13-06	–	–	.1	–	17	<.06	1.7	14	20
	06-20-07	S	–	<.1	–	18	<.06	1.8	44	9.7
	06-18-08	S	.1	.1	–	17	<.04	2.2	28	10
P1–6	06-08-99	S	1.8	0.1	–	–	–	0.12	0.02	–
	06-14-01	S	1.8	.2	34	34	0.23	.45	.95	4.9
	06-13-02	S	1.6	<.1	–	26	<.05	.88	1.0	4.3
	06-20-03	Fe	.3	.2	–	4.1	<.06	.08	.13	7.5
	06-18-04	S	1.5	.1	–	10	–	.11	1.0	7.2
	06-23-05	Fe/S	.3	.1	–	5.8	<.06	.17	.15	6.3
	06-13-06	S	1.1	.1	–	26	<.06	.91	1.4	3.4
	06-20-07	S	.2	<.1	–	3.9	<.06	.08	.08	7.1
	06-18-08	S	.2	.1	–	10	<.04	.15	.10	5.5
P1–7	06-08-99	S	1.2	0.1	–	–	–	0.61	2.1	–
	06-22-00	Mn/Fe	–	.1	19	–	–	2.6	3.2	24
	06-14-01	Mn/Fe	.2	.2	11	11	<0.05	2.3	2.0	18
	06-14-02	Mn/Fe	.2	1.3	–	8.9	<.05	2.2	1.9	12
	06-20-03	Mn/Fe	.1	.1	–	5.6	<.06	1.9	1.3	7.5
	06-18-04	Mn/Fe	.1	<.1	–	6.9	–	2.4	2.0	9.8
	06-22-05	Mn/Fe	<.1	.1	–	8.8	<.06	2.1	1.9	26
	06-13-06	Mn/Fe	<.1	.5	–	7.6	<.06	2.0	1.8	20
	06-20-07	Mn/Fe	.2	.1	–	5.7	<.06	2.1	1.18	6.0
	06-18-08	Mn/Fe	<.1	<.1	–	6.7	<.04	2.1	1.34	6.9

Table 2   23

Table 2. Predominant redox conditions at wells and piezometers, and groundwater geochemical data collected at Operable Unit 1, Naval Undersea Warfare Center, Division Keyport, Washington, 1996 to 2008.—Continued

[All other data were published in Dinicola and others (2002), Dinicola (2003), and Dinicola (2004); prior to 2000, bicarbonate was calculated from an unfiltered sample. Reported concentrations less than the detection limit usually are estimated. A range of dissolved hydrogen concentrations are shown when equilibration at a single value was never achieved. **Predominant redox conditions:** A, aerobic; An, anaerobic, but specific redox condition could not be determined; Fe, iron reducing; M, methanogenic; Mn, manganese reducing; N, nitrate reducing; S, sulfate reducing. **Abbreviations:** nM, nanomolar; mg/L, milligram per liter; µS/cm, microsiemens per centimeter at 25 degrees Celsius; ORP, oxidation-reduction potential; mV, millivolt. **Symbols**: E, estimated value; R, data rejected (selected 1996 dissolved-oxygen data were rejected because of inadequate well purging; selected 2002 dissolved-hydrogen data were rejected because of interference from downhole instruments); <, actual value is less than value shown; >, actual value is greater than value shown; –, not analyzed]

Well or piezometer No.	Date sampled	Predominant redox condition	Unfiltered sulfide (mg/L)	Dissolved methane (mg/L)	Dissolved carbon dioxide (mg/L)	Filtered bicarbonate (mg/L)	pH (units)	Specific conduc-tance (µS/cm)	ORP (mV)	Filtered chloride (mg/L)
				Southern Plantation—Continued						
MW1–16	09-17-96	S	<0.01	4.3	–	1,400	6.5	–	–	150
	04-16-97	Fe/S	.06	29	–	1,800	6.5	–	–	–
	03-04-98	Fe	.01	–	–	–	–	–	–	–
	10-08-98	M	<.01	–	–	1,600	6.3	3,370	–	–
	06-07-99	M	.01	–	–	1,200	6.7	1,820	–	–
	06-22-00	S	.02	1.2	–	510	6.7	902	-130	43
	06-14-01	S	.08	10	–	610	6.4	953	–	40
	06-13-02	M	.04	24	270	700	6.5	1,400	-140	17
	06-20-03	S	.06	9.7	240	–	6.5	835	–	6.8
	06-22-04	–	.50	4.3	230	–	6.3	817	–	6.9
	06-23-05	Fe/S	.12	–	225	–	6.6	767	-110	3.8
	06-13-06	–	.06	3.0	70	–	6.7	737	-139	3.5
	06-20-07	S	.13	2.1	190	–	6.4	763	-124	6 5
	06-18-08	S	.08	3.3	40	–	6.4	770	-62	16
P1–6	06-08-99	S	0.04	–	–	300	6.8	574	–	–
	06-14-01	S	12	6.3	–	350	6.4	657	-38	47
	06-13-02	S	11	11	170	380	6.4	604	-11	37
	06-20-03	Fe	.07	4.8	40	–	8.1	278	–	13
	06-18-04	S	10	.37	<10	–	8.6	268	–	18
	06-23-05	Fe/S	12	1.4	24	–	7.1	332	-53	24
	06-13-06	S	.14	2.6	30	–	6.6	757	-85	35
	06-20-07	S	.07	.38	16	–	8.3	249	-274	10
	06-18-08	S	.07	2.2	<10	–	8.3	291	218	22
P1-7	06-08-99	S	<0.01	–	–	310	6.7	627	–	–
	06-22-00	Mn/Fe	<.01	1.5	–	400	6.8	851	-35	55
	06-14-01	Mn/Fe	<.01	4.0	–	320	6.5	666	-32	41
	06-14-02	Mn/Fe	<.01	6 0	87	300	6.6	601	-41	60
	06-20-03	Mn/Fe	<.01	4.8	50	–	6.6	498	–	42
	06-18-04	Mn/Fe	<.01	1.7	40	–	6.7	613	–	56
	06-22-05	Mn/Fe	<.01	2.3	37	–	6.5	637	-20	55
	06-13-06	Mn/Fe	<.01	2.1	–	–	6.6	639	-60	49
	06-20-07	Mn/Fe	<.01	2.4	12	–	6.6	494	-57	43
	06-18-08	Mn/Fe	<.01	3.8	14	–	6.7	556	-18.9	49

Table 2. Predominant redox conditions at wells and piezometers, and groundwater geochemical data collected at Operable Unit 1, Naval Undersea Warfare Center, Division Keyport, Washington, 1996 to 2008.—Continued

[All other data were published in Dinicola and others (2002), Dinicola (2003), and Dinicola (2004); prior to 2000, bicarbonate was calculated from an unfiltered sample. Reported concentrations less than the detection limit usually are estimated. A range of dissolved hydrogen concentrations are shown when equilibration at a single value was never achieved. **Predominant redox conditions:** A, aerobic; An, anaerobic, but specific redox condition could not be determined; Fe, iron reducing; M, methanogenic; Mn, manganese reducing; N, nitrate reducing; S, sulfate reducing. **Abbreviations:** nM, nanomolar; mg/L, milligram per liter; µS/cm, microsiemens per centimeter at 25 degrees Celsius; ORP, oxidation-reduction potential; mV, millivolt. **Symbols**: E, estimated value; R, data rejected (selected 1996 dissolved-oxygen data were rejected because of inadequate well purging; selected 2002 dissolved-hydrogen data were rejected because of interference from downhole instruments); <, actual value is less than value shown; >, actual value is greater than value shown; –, not analyzed]

Well or piezometer No.	Date sampled	Predominant redox condition	Dissolved hydrogen (nM)	Dissolved oxygen (mg/L)	Unfiltered (total) organic carbon (mg/L)	Filtered (dissolved) organic carbon (mg/L)	Filtered nitrate + nitrite (mg/L as N)	Filtered manganese (mg/L)	Filtered iron (II) (mg/L)	Filtered sulfate (mg/L)
					Southern plantation—Continued					
P1–8	06-07-99	S	1.8	<0.1	–	–	–	0.20	0.08	–
	06-14-01	Fe	.7	.1	5	4.7	0.06	.16	.22	0.1
	06-13-02	Fe	.6	.3	–	8.8	<.05	.21	.38	.3
	06-20-03	Fe	.6	.1	–	2 3	<.06	.09	.12	.4
	06-18-04	Mn/Fe	.3	.4	–	3.0	–	.13	.01	.4
	06-23-05	Mn/Fe	.2	.2	–	14	<.06	.12	.12	<.2
	06-13-06	Mn/Fe	.3	<.1	–	3 2	<.06	.14	.02	.4
	06-20-07	M	.3	.1	–	3.9	<.06	.15	.14	<.18
	06-18-08	M	.1	<.1	–	4.1	<.04	.15	.16	.38
P1–9	06-08-99	M	19	0.3	–	–	–	0.90	0.03	–
	06-22-00	S/M	–	.1	10	–	–	.69	.20	6.6
	06-14-01	M	6.7	.1	2.3	1.7	<.05	.19	.05	7.6
	06-13-02	An	–	.6	–	9.8	<.05	1.2	.42	5.6
	06-20-03	Fe	.2	.1	–	3.7	<.06	.24	<.01	7.0
	06-18-04	Mn/Fe	.2	.1	–	4.0	–	.26	.14	7.3
	06-23-05	Mn	<.1	.1	–	1.4	<.06	.11	.01	8.7
	06-13-06	S	4.4	.2	–	9.6	<.06	1.4	.33	5.3
	06-20-07	Mn/Fe	.2	.1	–	4.5	<.06	.28	.13	7.04
	06-18-08	Mn/Fe	.1- 5	<.1	–	10	<.04	.17	.07	7.89
P1–10	06-07-99	Fe	0.7	0.3	–	–	–	0.10	0.11	–
	06-22-00	Fe	–	<.1	7.2	–	–	.07	.25	<0.3
	06-13-01	S	2.0	.2	3.0	4.2	<0.05	.07	.20	.06
	06-12-02	Fe	.3	.1	–	3 5	<.05	.05	.41	<.1
	06-19-03	Fe	.2	.1	–	3 5	<.06	.42	.34	2.6
	06-18-04	Mn/Fe	.1	.1	–	3.5	–	.58	.35	<.2
	06-22-05	Mn/Fe	.1	.1	–	3.3	<.06	.74	.24	<.2
	06-13-06	Mn/Fe	<.1	.1	–	3.4	<.06	.92	.15	<.2
	06-20-07	M	E.1	<.1	–	4.2	<.06	.10	.31	<.18
	06-18-08	M	<.1	<.1	–	4.2	<.04	.12	.23	<.18

Table 2   25

Table 2. Predominant redox conditions at wells and piezometers, and groundwater geochemical data collected at Operable Unit 1, Naval Undersea Warfare Center, Division Keyport, Washington, 1996 to 2008.—Continued

[All other data were published in Dinicola and others (2002), Dinicola (2003), and Dinicola (2004); prior to 2000, bicarbonate was calculated from an unfiltered sample. Reported concentrations less than the detection limit usually are estimated. A range of dissolved hydrogen concentrations are shown when equilibration at a single value was never achieved. **Predominant redox conditions:** A, aerobic; An, anaerobic, but specific redox condition could not be determined; Fe, iron reducing; M, methanogenic; Mn, manganese reducing; N, nitrate reducing; S, sulfate reducing. **Abbreviations:** nM, nanomolar; mg/L, milligram per liter; µS/cm, microsiemens per centimeter at 25 degrees Celsius; ORP, oxidation-reduction potential; mV, millivolt. **Symbols:** E, estimated value; R, data rejected (selected 1996 dissolved-oxygen data were rejected because of inadequate well purging; selected 2002 dissolved-hydrogen data were rejected because of interference from downhole instruments); <, actual value is less than value shown; >, actual value is greater than value shown; –, not analyzed]

Well or piezometer No.	Date sampled	Predominant redox condition	Unfiltered sulfide (mg/L)	Dissolved methane (mg/L)	Dissolved carbon dioxide (mg/L)	Filtered bicarbonate (mg/L)	pH (units)	Specific conduc- tance (µS/cm)	ORP (mV)	Filtered chloride (mg/L)
				Southern Plantation—Continued						
P1-8	06-07-99	S	0.01	–	–	210	7.6	381	–	–
	06-14-01	Fe	.02	6.9	–	200	7.0	363	-73	18
	06-13-02	Fe	.02	11	40	104	6.9	482	-46	35
	06-20-03	Fe	<.01	9.6	<10	–	7.2	285	–	3.3
	06-18-04	Mn/Fe	.01	1.7	<10	–	7.4	336	-218	5.9
	06-23-05	Mn/Fe	<.01	3.4	<10	–	7.5	308	-147	4.2
	06-13-06	Mn/Fe	<.01	4.5	<10	–	7.5	332	-124	8.0
	06-20-07	M	<.01	6.6	9	–	7.5	348	-149	5.9
	06-18-08	M	<.01	7.9	<10	–	8.0	358	-136	8.7
P1-9	06-08-99	M	<0.01	–	–	270	6.6	680	–	–
	06-22-00	S/M	<.01	1.7	–	250	6.8	548	-17	59
	06-14-01	M	<.01	1.4	–	200	7.8	289	-120	14
	06-13-02	An	<.01	7.5	91	280	6.5	601	17	71
	06-20-03	Fe	.01	2.5	27	–	7.0	353	–	23
	06-18-04	Mn/Fe	<.01	.71	35	–	6.7	330	-97	26
	06-23-05	Mn	<.01	.02	<10	–	8.3	202	22	12
	06-13-06	S	.01	3.2	37	–	6.6	728	-9	112
	06-20-07	Mn/Fe	<.01	1.4	10	–	7.4	325	-110	31
	06-18-08	Mn/Fe	<.01	.74	<10	–	7.6	235	–	28
P1-10	06-07-99	Fe	<0.01	–	–	300	6.7	560	–	–
	06-22-00	Fe	<.01	1.3	–	290	7.1	500	-19	15
	06-13-01	S	<.01	4.9	–	290	7.2	476	-24	15
	06-12-02	Fe	<.01	18	51	270	6.8	438	8	14
	06-19-03	Fe	<.01	8.2	30	–	6.6	425	–	16
	06-18-04	Mn/Fe	<.01	33	45		6.3	422	-69	9.5
	06-23-05	Mn/Fe	<.01	.71	40	–	6.6	420	4	11
	06-13-06	Mn/Fe	<.01	6.3	29	–	6.6	437	-15	26
	06-20-07	M	<.01	6.1	15	–	6.3	391	-21	15
	06-18-08	M	<.01	4.7	11	–	6.8	358	14	7.3

Table 2. Predominant redox conditions at wells and piezometers, and groundwater geochemical data collected at Operable Unit 1, Naval Undersea Warfare Center, Division Keyport, Washington, 1996 to 2008.—Continued

[All other data were published in Dinicola and others (2002), Dinicola (2003), and Dinicola (2004); prior to 2000, bicarbonate was calculated from an unfiltered sample. Reported concentrations less than the detection limit usually are estimated. A range of dissolved hydrogen concentrations are shown when equilibration at a single value was never achieved. **Predominant redox conditions:** A, aerobic; An, anaerobic, but specific redox condition could not be determined; Fe, iron reducing; M, methanogenic; Mn, manganese reducing; N, nitrate reducing; S, sulfate reducing. **Abbreviations:** nM, nanomolar; mg/L, milligram per liter; µS/cm, microsiemens per centimeter at 25 degrees Celsius; ORP, oxidation-reduction potential; mV, millivolt. **Symbols:** E, estimated value; R, data rejected (selected 1996 dissolved-oxygen data were rejected because of inadequate well purging; selected 2002 dissolved-hydrogen data were rejected because of interference from downhole instruments); <, actual value is less than value shown; >, actual value is greater than value shown; –, not analyzed]

Well or piezometer No.	Date sampled	Predominant redox condition	Dissolved hydrogen (nM)	Dissolved oxygen (mg/L)	Unfiltered (total) organic carbon (mg/L)	Filtered (dissolved) organic carbon (mg/L)	Filtered nitrate + nitrite (mg/L as N)	Filtered manganese (mg/L)	Filtered iron (II) (mg/L)	Filtered sulfate (mg/L)
					Intermediate aquifer					
MW1–25	09-17-96	Fe	0.4	2.7R	7.4	–	0.14	0.16	0.74	16
	04-17-97	Fe	.8	.1	–	–	<.02	–	.88	15
	03-05-98	Fe	.3	.3	7.9	–	–	.20	.73	–
	10-05-98	Fe	.2	.1	–	–	–	.19	.99	–
	06-22-00	Fe	.4	.2	6.5	–	–	.16	.80	13
	06-12-01	S	2.8–4.3	.2	7.1	6.8	<.05	.16	.99	13
	06-14-02	S	0.7–2.4	.1	–	6.2	<.05	.18	1.1	9.7
	06-19-03	Fe	.3	.1	–	6.5	<.06	.18	1.1	11
	06-16-04	Fe	.2	.1	–	6.2	–	.17	1.0	10
	06-21-05	Fe	.1	.1	–	5.9	<.06	.16	1.0	9.5
	06-14-06	Fe	.1	.1	–	6.3	<.06	.14	.97	8.1
	06-18-07	Fe	.2	<.1	–	6.6	<.06	.14	.87	7.1
	06-17-08	Fe	<.1	.1	–	6.4	<.04	.13	.86	6.9
MW1–28	09-16-96	Fe	0.3	2.1R	7.2	–	<0.02	0.20	1.0	48
	04-17-97	Fe	1.0	<.1	–	–	.04	–	.99	51
	03-05-98	Fe	.4	.5	7.7	–	–	.20	.67	–
	10-07-98	Fe	.6	<.1	–	–	–	.19	1.0	–
	06-22-00	Fe	.3	<.1	13	–	–	.16	.66	44
	06-12-01	S/M	4.1–5.7	.5	10	6.9	<.05	.16	.90	45
	06-14-02	An	>100R	.1	–	7.0	<.05	.16	.92	39
	06-19-03	S	2.5	.1	–	6.8	<.06	.16	.66	39
	06-16-04	Mn/Fe	.2	.1	–	5.9	–	.18	<.01	36
	06-21-05	Fe	.1	.2	–	6.3	<.06	.16	.98	37
	06-14-06	Fe	.1	.1	–	6.1	<.06	.16	.78	35
	06-18-07	Fe	.1	<.1	–	6.7	<.06	.16	.87	33
	06-17-08	Fe	.1	<.1	–	7.1	<.04	.15	.85	33
MW1–38	10-09-98	Fe	–	0.1	–	–	–	0.20	0.08	–
	06-20-00	Fe	0.1	.2	5.6	–	<0.05	.08	.10	2.3
	06-12-02	S	1.4	<.1	5.0	–	<.05	.08	.42	2.9
	06-16-04	Mn/Fe	.2	.1	–	4.9	–	.06	.04	1.2
	06-24-05	Fe	.3	.1	–	4.4	<.06	.06	.09	3.3
	06-14-06	Mn/Fe	.1	.1	–	2.4	<.06	.01	.05	1.0
	06-21-07	S	.2	.6	–	4.7	<.06	.04	.04	3.1
	06-17-08	S	<.1	.1	–	5.0	<.04	.04	.03	2.5

Table 2   27

Table 2. Predominant redox conditions at wells and piezometers, and groundwater geochemical data collected at Operable Unit 1, Naval Undersea Warfare Center, Division Keyport, Washington, 1996 to 2008.—Continued

[All other data were published in Dinicola and others (2002), Dinicola (2003), and Dinicola (2004); prior to 2000, bicarbonate was calculated from an unfiltered sample. Reported concentrations less than the detection limit usually are estimated. A range of dissolved hydrogen concentrations are shown when equilibration at a single value was never achieved. **Predominant redox conditions:** A, aerobic; An, anaerobic, but specific redox condition could not be determined; Fe, iron reducing; M, methanogenic; Mn, manganese reducing; N, nitrate reducing; S, sulfate reducing. **Abbreviations:** nM, nanomolar; mg/L, milligram per liter; µS/cm, microsiemens per centimeter at 25 degrees Celsius; ORP, oxidation-reduction potential; mV, millivolt. **Symbols:** E, estimated value; R, data rejected (selected 1996 dissolved-oxygen data were rejected because of inadequate well purging; selected 2002 dissolved-hydrogen data were rejected because of interference from downhole instruments); <, actual value is less than value shown; >, actual value is greater than value shown; –, not analyzed]

Well or piezometer No.	Date sampled	Predominant redox condition	Unfiltered sulfide (mg/L)	Dissolved methane (mg/L)	Dissolved carbon dioxide (mg/L)	Filtered bicarbonate (mg/L)	pH (units)	Specific conductance (µS/cm)	ORP (mV)	Filtered chloride (mg/L)
					Intermediate aquifer					
MW1-25	09-17-96	Fe	<0.01	3.6	–	360	7.1	–	–	140
	04-17-97	Fe	<.01	7.9	–	1,000	7.0	–	–	–
	03-05-98	Fe	<.01	–	–	–	–	–	–	–
	10-05-98	Fe	<.01	–	–	450	6.9	1,240	–	–
	06-22-00	Fe	<.01	.79	–	380	6.9	1,230	-49	170
	06-12-01	S	<.01	4.7	–	440	6.7	1,180	-36	160
	06-14-02	S	<.01	7.0	83	370	6.7	1,030	-60	170
	06-19-03	Fe	<.01	8.1	65	–	6.7	1,180	-17	170
	06-16-04	Fe	<.01	1.4	40	–	7.1	1,210	-	160
	06-21-05	Fe	<.01	2.1	33	–	6.9	1,150	-9	160
	06-14-06	Fe	<.01	2.4	27	–	6.9	1,090	-71	140
	06-18-07	Fe	<.01	1.3	27	–	6.6	1,040	-152	140
	06-17-08	Fe	<.01	2.8	35	–	6.9	1,040	-45	140
MW1-28	09-16-96	Fe	<0.01	1.7	–	350	–	–	–	380
	04-17-97	Fe	<.01	5.3	–	1,100	7.4	–	–	–
	03-05-98	Fe	<.01	–	–	–	–	–	–	–
	10-07-98	Fe	.02	–	–	320	6.6	2,630	–	–
	06-22-00	Fe	<.01	.45	–	480	7.3	2,460	-87	510
	06-12-01	S/M	<.01	4.1	–	480	7.4	2,200	-220	490
	06-14-02	An	<.01	3.9	40	470	7.2	2,580	-110	460
	06-19-03	S	<.01	1.7	32	–	7.1	2,440	-40	490
	06-16-04	Mn/Fe	<.01	.77	21	–	7.2	2,280	–	450
	06-21-05	Fe	<.01	1.0	23	–	6.9	2,210	-124	472
	06-14-06	Fe	.01	.83	21	–	7.0	2,110	-127	443
	06-18-07	Fe	.02	.67	25	–	7.1	2,060	–	430
	06-17-08	Fe	<.01	1.5	13	–	7.1	2,080	-112	420
MW1-38	10-09-98	Fe	0.02	–	–	310	7.8	1,460	–	–
	06-20-00	Fe	.03	0.10	–	300	7.8	1,240	-130	230
	06-12-02	S	.04	1.1	7.7	310	7.6	1,350	-160	230
	06-16-04	Mn/Fe	.03	.13	11	–	7.4	1,130	–	200
	06-24-05	Fe	.03	.05	<10	–	7.7	1,210	-116	230
	06-14-06	Mn/Fe	<.01	.41	<10	–	7.5	1,120	-55	62
	06-21-07	S	.05	.31	9.0	–	7.4	1,190	-114	230
	06-17-08	S	.02	.32	<10	–	7.7	1,140	-43	220

Table 2.   Predominant redox conditions at wells and piezometers, and groundwater geochemical data collected at Operable Unit 1, Naval Undersea Warfare Center, Division Keyport, Washington, 1996 to 2008.—Continued

[All other data were published in Dinicola and others (2002), Dinicola (2003), and Dinicola (2004); prior to 2000, bicarbonate was calculated from an unfiltered sample. Reported concentrations less than the detection limit usually are estimated. A range of dissolved hydrogen concentrations are shown when equilibration at a single value was never achieved. **Predominant redox conditions:** A, aerobic; An, anaerobic, but specific redox condition could not be determined; Fe, iron reducing; M, methanogenic; Mn, manganese reducing; N, nitrate reducing; S, sulfate reducing. **Abbreviations:** nM, nanomolar; mg/L, milligram per liter; μS/cm, microsiemens per centimeter at 25 degrees Celsius; ORP, oxidation-reduction potential; mV, millivolt. **Symbols**: E, estimated value; R, data rejected (selected 1996 dissolved-oxygen data were rejected because of inadequate well purging; selected 2002 dissolved-hydrogen data were rejected because of interference from downhole instruments); <, actual value is less than value shown; >, actual value is greater than value shown; –, not analyzed]

Well or piezometer No.	Date sampled	Predominant redox condition	Dissolved hydrogen (nM)	Dissolved oxygen (mg/L)	Unfiltered (total) organic carbon (mg/L)	Filtered (dissolved) organic carbon (mg/L)	Filtered nitrate + nitrite (mg/L as N)	Filtered manganese (mg/L)	Filtered iron (II) (mg/L)	Filtered sulfate (mg/L)
					Intermediate aquifer—Continued					
MW1–39	09-16-96	Fe/S	0.6	2.0R	4.4	–	<0.02	0.02	<0.01	0.7
	04-17-97	S	4.5	<.1	–	–	<.02	–	.05	13
	03-03-98	Fe/S	.3	.3	3.7	–	–	.10	.03	–
	10-09-98	Fe/S	.5	<.1	–	–	–	<.01	.04	–
	06-07-99	Fe/S	1.0	.3	–	–	–	.10	.02	–
	06-20-00	Fe/S	.5	.1	2.4	–	<.05	.01	.07	.2
	06-12-01	S	1.4	.3	3.4	3 3	<.05	.01	<.01	.1
	06-12-02	M	>30R	<.1	–	2.8	<.05	.01	.10	.1
	06-19-03	S	1.8	.1	–	2 5	<.06	.01	<.01	1.2
	06-16-04	S	2.0	.1	–	2.4	–	.01	.05	.1
	06-14-06	Fe/S	.7	.1	–	4.5	<.06	.05	.05	1.7
	06-21-07	S	1.0	<.1	–	2.3	<.06	.01	.04	.98
	06-17-08	S	1.8	.6	–	2.7	<.04	.01	.04	1.0

Table 2   29

Table 2.   Predominant redox conditions at wells and piezometers, and groundwater geochemical data collected at Operable Unit 1, Naval Undersea Warfare Center, Division Keyport, Washington, 1996 to 2008.—Continued

[All other data were published in Dinicola and others (2002), Dinicola (2003), and Dinicola (2004); prior to 2000, bicarbonate was calculated from an unfiltered sample. Reported concentrations less than the detection limit usually are estimated. A range of dissolved hydrogen concentrations are shown when equilibration at a single value was never achieved. **Predominant redox conditions:** A, aerobic; An, anaerobic, but specific redox condition could not be determined; Fe, iron reducing; M, methanogenic; Mn, manganese reducing; N, nitrate reducing; S, sulfate reducing. **Abbreviations:** nM, nanomolar; mg/L, milligram per liter; µS/cm, microsiemens per centimeter at 25 degrees Celsius; ORP, oxidation-reduction potential; mV, millivolt. **Symbols:** E, estimated value; R, data rejected (selected 1996 dissolved-oxygen data were rejected because of inadequate well purging; selected 2002 dissolved-hydrogen data were rejected because of interference from downhole instruments); <, actual value is less than value shown; >, actual value is greater than value shown; –, not analyzed]

Well or piezometer No.	Date sampled	Predominant redox condition	Unfiltered sulfide (mg/L)	Dissolved methane (mg/L)	Dissolved carbon dioxide (mg/L)	Filtered bicarbonate (mg/L)	pH (units)	Specific conduc- tance (µS/cm)	ORP (mV)	Filtered chloride (mg/L)
				Intermediate aquifer—Continued						
MW1–39	09-16-96	Fe/S	0.04	1.6	–	140	–	–	–	85
	04-17-97	S	.06	6.1	–	360	7.9	–	–	–
	03-03-98	Fe/S	.05	–	–	–	–	–	–	–
	10-09-98	Fe/S	.07	–	–	170	8.1	502	–	–
	06-07-99	Fe/S	<.01	–	–	180	8.0	512	–	–
	06-20-00	Fe/S	.08	.41	–	180	8.0	481	-130	61
	06-12-01	S	.05	2.7	–	170	7.8	472	-130	61
	06-12-02	M	.06	4.8	2.4	180	7.9	464	-120	60
	06-19-03	S	.05	5.4	<10	–	7.7	456	32	58
	06-16-04	S	.07	.72	<10	–	7.4	451	-216	58
	06-14-06	Fe/S	.06	1.2	<10	–	8.0	461	-138	210
	06-21-07	S	.05	1.3	<10	–	7.7	453	-195	60
	06-17-08	S	.06	1.9	<10	–	7.9	451	-163	59

Table 3.   Concentrations of selected volatile organic compounds in groundwater samples from monitoring wells and piezometers collected by the U.S. Geological Survey at Operable Unit 1, Naval Undersea Warfare Center, Division Keyport, Washington., 1999–2008.

[All data except those shaded were published previously in Dinicola and others (2002), Dinicola (2003), Dinicola (2004), and Dinicola and Huffman (2004). Laboratory data qualifier codes, such as "D" for dilution, are not shown. **Volatile organic compounds (VOCs)**; PCE, tetrachloroethene; TCE, trichloroethene; *cis*-DCE, *cis*-1,2-dichloroethene; *trans*-DCE, *trans*-1,2-dichloroethene; VC, vinyl chloride; 1,1,1-TCA, 1,1,1-trichloroethane; 1,1-DCA, 1,1-dichloroethane; CA, chloroethane; 1,1-DCE, 1,1-dichloroethene; total BTEX, sum of benzene, toluene, ethylbenzene, and xylene; total CVOCs, sum of chlorinated volatile organic compounds. **Abbreviations:** E, estimated value; M, presence verified but not quantified; µg/L, microgram per liter; dup, duplicate; blank, field blank; <, actual value is less than value shown; ND, not detected; –, not analyzed]

Well or piezometer No.	Date sampled	PCE (µg/L)	TCE (µg/L)	*cis*-DCE (µg/L)	*trans*-DCE (µg/L)	VC (µg/L)	Ethane (µg/L)	Ethene (µg/L)
				Upgradient				
MW1-3	06-20-00	–	–	–	–	–	–	0.12
	06-15-04	–	–	–	–	–	<5.0	<5.0
	06-12-06	–	–	–	–	–	<5.0	<5.0
MW1-20	06-21-00	–	–	–	–	–	–	<.10
	06-12-02	<0.20	<0.20	<0.20	<0.20	<0.20	–	–
	06-15-04	–	–	–	–	–	<5.0	<5.0
	06-13-06	–	–	–	–	–	<5.0	<5.0
MW1-33	06-21-00	–	–	–	–	–	–	.18
	06-15-04	–	–	–	–	–	<5.0	<5.0
	06-12-06	–	–	–	–	–	<5.0	<5.0
				Northern plantation				
1MW-1	06-21-00	–	–	–	–	–	–	8.6
	06-16-04	<20	<20	130	130	730	E10	50
	06-12-06	–	–	–	–	–	E21	61
	06-19-07	–	–	–	–	–	E9.0	E38
	06-17-08	–	–	–	–	–	E47	110
MW1-2	06-21-00	–	–	–	–	–	–	0.26
	06-18-03	<2.0	<2.0	58	4.0	79	–	–
	06-17-04	<50	E12	630	E13	110	6.0	E1.1
	06-12-06	–	–	–	–	–	5.0	<5.0
	06-19-07	–	–	–	–	–	E4.0	<5.0
	06-17-08	–	–	–	–	–	7.0	E.70
MW1-17	06-22-00	–	–	–	–	–	–	<0.10
	06-17-04	<1.0	<1.0	E0.68	E0.23	E0.48	E2.0	<5.0
	06-20-07	–	–	–	–	–	E11	<50
	06-18-08	–	–	–	–	–	E17	E13
MW1-41	06-21-00	–	–	–	–	–	–	<0.10
	06-17-04	<1.0	<1.0	E0.27	<1.0	E0.23	E10	<100
	06-12-06	–	–	–	–	–	<100	<100
	06-19-07	–	–	–	–	–	<100	<100
	06-16-08	–	–	–	–	–	<120	<120

Table 3   31

Table 3. Concentrations of selected volatile organic compounds in groundwater samples from monitoring wells and piezometers collected by the U.S. Geological Survey at Operable Unit 1, Naval Undersea Warfare Center, Division Keyport, Washington, 1999–2008.—Continued

[All data except those shaded were published previously in Dinicola and others (2002), Dinicola (2003), Dinicola (2004), and Dinicola and Huffman (2004). Laboratory data qualifier codes, such as "D" for dilution, are not shown. **Volatile organic compounds (VOCs)**: PCE, tetrachloroethene; TCE, trichloroethene; cis-DCE, cis-1,2-dichloroethene; trans-DCE, trans-1,2-dichloroethene; VC, vinyl chloride; 1,1,1-TCA, 1,1,1-trichloroethane; 1,1-DCA, 1,1-dichloroethane; CA, chloroethane; 1,1-DCE, 1,1-dichloroethene; total BTEX, sum of benzene, toluene, ethylbenzene, and xylene; total CVOCs, sum of chlorinated volatile organic compounds. **Abbreviations:** E, estimated value; M, presence verified but not quantified; μg/L, microgram per liter; dup, duplicate; blank, field blank; <, actual value is less than value shown; ND, not detected; –, not analyzed]

Well or piezometer No.	Date sampled	1,1,1-TCA (μg/L)	1,1-DCA (μg/L)	CA (μg/L)	1,1-DCE (μg/L)	Total BTEX (μg/L)	Total CVOCs (μg/L)
				Upgradient			
MW1-3	06-20-00	–	–	–	–	–	–
	06-15-04	–	–	–	–	–	–
	06-12-06	–	–	–	–	–	–
MW1-20	06-21-00	–	–	–	–	–	–
	06-12-02	<0.20	<0.20	<0.20	<0.20	ND	ND
	06-15-04	–	–	–	–	–	–
	06-13-06	–	–	–	–	–	–
MW1-33	06-21-00	–	–	–	–	–	–
	06-15-04	–	–	–	–	–	–
	06-12-06	–	–	–	–	–	–
				Northern plantation			
1MW-1	06-21-00	–	–	–	–	–	–
	06-16-04	<20	E11	<40	<20	ND	880
	06-12-06	–	–	–	–	–	–
	06-19-07	–	–	–	–	–	–
	06-17-08	–	–	–	–	–	–
MW1-2	06-21-00	–	–	–	–	–	–
	06-18-03	<2.0	M	5.0	<2.0	E2.0	150
	06-17-04	<50	<50	<100	<50	ND	760
	06-12-06	–	–	–	–	–	–
	06-19-07	–	–	–	–	–	–
	06-17-08	–	–	–	–	–	–
MW1-17	06-22-00	–	–	–	–	–	–
	06-17-04	<1.0	<1.0	<2.0	<1.0	E3.1	E1.4
	06-20-07	–	–	–	–	–	–
	06-18-08	–	–	–	–	–	–
MW1-41	06-21-00	–	–	–	–	–	–
	06-17-04	<1.0	<1.0	E1.7	<1.0	E.27	E2.2
	06-12-06	–	–	–	–	–	–
	06-19-07	–	–	–	–	–	–
	06-16-08	–	–	–	–	–	–

Table 3.   Concentrations of selected volatile organic compounds in groundwater samples from monitoring wells and piezometers collected by the U.S. Geological Survey at Operable Unit 1, Naval Undersea Warfare Center, Division Keyport, Washington, 1999–2008. —Continued

[All data except those shaded were published previously in Dinicola and others (2002), Dinicola (2003), Dinicola (2004), and Dinicola and Huffman (2004). Laboratory data qualifier codes, such as "D" for dilution, are not shown. **Volatile organic compounds (VOCs)**; PCE, tetrachloroethene; TCE, trichloroethene; *cis*-DCE, *cis*-1,2-dichloroethene; *trans*-DCE, *trans*-1,2-dichloroethene; VC, vinyl chloride; 1,1,1-TCA, 1,1,1-trichloroethane; 1,1-DCA, 1,1-dichloroethane; CA, chloroethane; 1,1-DCE, 1,1-dichloroethene; total BTEX, sum of benzene, toluene, ethylbenzene, and xylene; total CVOCs, sum of chlorinated volatile organic compounds. **Abbreviations:** E, estimated value; M, presence verified but not quantified; µg/L, microgram per liter; dup, duplicate; blank, field blank; <, actual value is less than value shown; ND, not detected; –, not analyzed]

Well or piezometer No.	Date sampled	PCE (µg/L)	TCE (µg/L)	*cis*-DCE (µg/L)	*trans*-DCE (µg/L)	VC (µg/L)	Ethane (µg/L)	Ethene (µg/L)
				Northern plantation—Continued				
P1-1	06-09-99	<2.0	11	6.1	<1.0	<4.0	–	–
	06-11-02	<.20	<.20	.20	.10	<.20	–	–
	06-18-03	<1.0	<1.0	E.30	<1.0	<1.0	–	–
	06-17-04	<1.0	<1.0	<1.0	<1.0	<1.0	E29	E8.6
	06-22-05	<1.0	<1.0	E.16	<1.0	<1.0	<100	<100
	06-12-06	<1.0	<1.0	<1.0	<1.0	<1.0	<100	<100
	06-19-07	–	–	–	–	–	<100	<100
	06-16-08	<1.0	<1.0	E.18	<1.0	<2.0	<250	<250
P1-3	06-09-99	<16	35	450	20	120	–	–
	06-11-02	<.20	<.20	53	4.3	72	–	–
	06-18-03	<2.0	<2.0	58	4.0	79	–	–
	06-17-04	<1.0	<1.0	15	2.4	41	E33	E27
	06-22-05	<1.0	<1.0	11	1.3	35	E44	E30
	06-12-06	<1.0	<1.0	4.6	1.2	16	E35	E21
	06-19-07	<1.0	<1.0	1.8	1.0	15	E42	E27
	06-17-08	<1.0	<1.0	E.17	E.31	E.67	E64	E20
P1-4	06-09-99	<130	160	4,800	56	540	–	–
	06-13-01	<20	<20	4,900	46	652	–	–
	06-11-02	<.20	1.2	3,600	41	640	–	–
	06-18-03	<100	<100	3,200	E42	440	–	–
	06-17-04	<130	<130	2,300	E29	370	E7.0	E29
	06-21-05	<67	<67	2,100	E30	360	E7.0	E20
	06-12-06	<50	<50	1,600	E24	280	E6.0	E19
	06-19-07	<40	<40	15,00	E24	280	E11	E29
	06-16-08	<50	<50	1,600	E24	750	E14	E29
P1-5	06-08-99	<13	440	400	4.0	11	–	–
	06-10-02	<.20	<.20	.30	.80	.40	–	–
	06-18-03	<25	<25	E7.8	<25	<25	–	–
	06-17-04	<10	<10	<10	<10	<10	23	<10
	06-21-05	<10	<10	<10	<10	<10	E23	<100
	06-12-06	<10	<10	<10	<10	<10	E16	<100
	06-19-07	–	–	–	–	–	E19	<100
	06-16-08	<50	<50	<50	<50	<100	E45	<100
				Southern plantation				
MW1-4	06-22-00	–	–	–	–	–	–	12
	06-18-04	<1,000	32,000	15,000	<1,000	1,600	E32	200
	06-13-06	–	–	–	–	–	E39	200
	06-20-07	–	–	–	–	–	6.0	32
	06-18-08	–	–	–	–	–	30	120

Table 3   33

Table 3. Concentrations of selected volatile organic compounds in groundwater samples from monitoring wells and piezometers collected by the U.S. Geological Survey at Operable Unit 1, Naval Undersea Warfare Center, Division Keyport, Washington, 1999–2008. —Continued

[All data except those shaded were published previously in Dinicola and others (2002), Dinicola (2003), Dinicola (2004), and Dinicola and Huffman (2004). Laboratory data qualifier codes, such as "D" for dilution, are not shown. **Volatile organic compounds (VOCs)**; PCE, tetrachloroethene; TCE, trichloroethene; *cis*-DCE, *cis*-1,2-dichloroethene; *trans*-DCE, *trans*-1,2-dichloroethene; VC, vinyl chloride; 1,1,1-TCA, 1,1,1-trichloroethane; 1,1-DCA, 1,1-dichloroethane; CA, chloroethane; 1,1-DCE, 1,1-dichloroethene; total BTEX, sum of benzene, toluene, ethylbenzene, and xylene; total CVOCs, sum of chlorinated volatile organic compounds. **Abbreviations:** E, estimated value; M, presence verified but not quantified; μg/L, microgram per liter; dup, duplicate; blank, field blank; <, actual value is less than value shown; ND, not detected; –, not analyzed]

Well or piezometer No.	Date sampled	1,1,1-TCA (μg/L)	1,1-DCA (μg/L)	CA (μg/L)	1,1-DCE (μg/L)	Total BTEX (μg/L)	Total CVOCs (μg/L)
			Northern plantation—Continued				
P1-1	06-09-99	<2.0	M	<4.0	<2.0	18	17
	06-11-02	<.20	0.50	<.20	<.20	6.8	.80
	06-18-03	<1.0	M	<2.0	<1.0	4.0	E.30
	06-17-04	<1.0	<1.0	<2.0	<1.0	4.4	ND
	06-22-05	<1.0	<1.0	E.19	<1.0	3.5	.35
	06-12-06	<1.0	<1.0	<2.0	<1.0	3.1	ND
	06-19-07	–	–	–	–	–	–
	06-16-08	<1.0	<1.0	<2.0	<1.0	3.9	E.18
P1-3	06-09-99	<16	<16	4.0	<16	ND	630
	06-11-02	<.20	.60	9.9	.20	3.3	140
	06-18-03	<2.0	M	5.0	<2.0	E2.0	150
	06-17-04	<1.0	E.38	6.9	<1.0	2.4	66
	06-22-05	<1.0	E.31	2.6	<1.0	2.3	50
	06-12-06	<1.0	E.32	4.4	<1.0	2.2	26
	06-19-07	<1.0	E.42	5.6	<1.0	2.2	24
	06-17-08	<1.0	E.24	9.1	<1.0	3.9	10
P1-4	06-09-99	<130	<130	<270	<130	ND	5,600
	06-13-01	<20	<20	<20	<20	ND	5,600
	06-11-02	<.20	<10	.80	9.9	1.1	4,300
	06-18-03	<100	<100	<200	<100	ND	3,700
	06-17-04	<130	<130	<270	<130	ND	2,700
	06-21-05	<67	<67	<130	<67	ND	2,500
	06-12-06	<50	<50	<100	<50	ND	1,900
	06-19-07	<40	<40	<80	<40	66	1,800
	06-16-08	<50	<50	<100	<50	ND	2,400
P1-5	06-08 99	<13	<13	15	<13	47	470
	06-10-02	<.20	.30	21	<.20	18	23
	06-18-03	<25	<25	E19	<25	ND	E27
	06-17-04	<10	<10	23	<10	E4.5	23
	06-21-05	<10	<10	21	<10	8.2	21
	06-12-06	<10	<10	E14	<10	E4.2	E14
	06-19-07	–	–	–	–	–	–
	06-16-08	<50	<50	<100	<50	ND	ND
			Southern plantation				
MW1-4	06-22-00	–	–	–	–	–	–
	06-18-04	<1,000	<1,000	<2,000	<1,000	ND	49,000
	06-13-06	–	–	–	–	–	–
	06-20-07	–	–	–	–	–	–
	06-18-08	–	–	–	–	–	–

Table 3.   Concentrations of selected volatile organic compounds in groundwater samples from monitoring wells and piezometers collected by the U.S. Geological Survey at Operable Unit 1, Naval Undersea Warfare Center, Division Keyport, Washington, 1999–2008. —Continued

[All data except those shaded were published previously in Dinicola and others (2002), Dinicola (2003), Dinicola (2004), and Dinicola and Huffman (2004). Laboratory data qualifier codes, such as "D" for dilution, are not shown. **Volatile organic compounds (VOCs)**; PCE, tetrachloroethene; TCE, trichloroethene; *cis*-DCE, *cis*-1,2-dichloroethene; *trans*-DCE, *trans*-1,2-dichloroethene; VC, vinyl chloride; 1,1,1-TCA, 1,1,1-trichloroethane; 1,1-DCA, 1,1-dichloroethane; CA, chloroethane; 1,1-DCE, 1,1-dichloroethene; total BTEX, sum of benzene, toluene, ethylbenzene, and xylene; total CVOCs, sum of chlorinated volatile organic compounds. **Abbreviations:** E, estimated value; M, presence verified but not quantified; µg/L, microgram per liter; dup, duplicate; blank, field blank; <, actual value is less than value shown; ND, not detected; –, not analyzed]

Well or piezometer No.	Date sampled	PCE (µg/L)	TCE (µg/L)	*cis*-DCE (µg/L)	*trans*-DCE (µg/L)	VC (µg/L)	Ethane (µg/L)	Ethene (µg/L)
				Southern plantation—Continued				
MW1-5	06-22-00	–	–	–	–	–	–	8.6
	06-18-04	<1.0	E0.26	E0.29	<1.0	E0.74	E7.0	<50
	06-13-06	–	–	–	–	–	E9.0	E30
	06-20-07	–	–	–	–	–	E3.0	<25
	06-18-08	–	–	–	–	–	E6.0	E7.2
MW1-16	06-22-00	–	–	–	–	–	–	70
	06-22-04	<10	<10	E2.3	E4.2	E2.2	E38	E33
	06-13-06	–	–	–	–	–	E23	E6.8
	06-20-07	–	–	–	–	–	E24	E18
	06-18-08	–	–	–	–	–	E19	E6.3
P1-6	06-08-99	<400	74	16,000	170	5,400	–	–
	06-14-01	<20	370	16,000	220	9,900	–	–
	06-13-02	<20	<20	3,700	170	5,100	–	–
	06-20-03	<50	470	1,100	E39	1,300	–	–
	06-18-04	<20	<20	220	E11	570	7.0	210
	06-22-05	<130	<130	4,200	E90	2,900	E30	590
	06-13-06	<100	<100	300	E77	770	82	1,300
	06-20-07	<8.0	<8.0	84	E5.4	140	7.0	180
	06-18-08	<200	<200	8,800	E130	9,700	57	720
P1-7	06-08-99	<670	26,000	35,000	210	3,100	–	–
	06-22-00	3.6	27,000	44,000	220	3,800	–	68
	06-14-01	<20	26,000	37,000	190	4,000	–	–
	06-14-02	<20	37,000	62,000	400	5,700	–	–
	06-20-03	<2,000	28,000	35,000	<2000	2,800	–	–
	06-18-04	<3,300	37,000	61,000	<3300	5,100	E36	520
	06-22-05	<2,000	28,000	59,000	E330	5,000	E45	480
	06-13-06	<2,000	24,000	43,000	<2000	3,800	E44	400
	06-20-07	<2,000	33,000	44,000	E320	4,000	E47	460
	06-18-08	<2,000	38,000	65,000	E370	14,000	88	850
P1-8	06-07-99	<710	190	25,000	210	3,400	–	–
	06-14-01	<20	810	8,600	62	4,200	–	–
	06-13-02	<20	<20	24,000	190	7,700	–	–
	06-20-03	<10	230	31	<10	E7.0	–	–
	06-18-04	<1.0	E.26	2.7	<1.0	23	<50	E4.2
	06-23-05	<1.0	<1.0	7.0	<1.0	21	<50	<50
	06-13-06	<20	<20	620	E4.0	58	<50	E9.5
	06-20-07	<4.0	E2.4	29	<4.0	41	<100	E13
	06-18-08	<10	<10	160	<10	280	E6.0	E16

Table 3   35

Table 3. Concentrations of selected volatile organic compounds in groundwater samples from monitoring wells and piezometers collected by the U.S. Geological Survey at Operable Unit 1, Naval Undersea Warfare Center, Division Keyport, Washington, 1999–2008. —Continued

[All data except those shaded were published previously in Dinicola and others (2002), Dinicola (2003), Dinicola (2004), and Dinicola and Huffman (2004). Laboratory data qualifier codes, such as "D" for dilution, are not shown. **Volatile organic compounds (VOCs)**: PCE, tetrachloroethene; TCE, trichloroethene; *cis*-DCE, *cis*-1,2-dichloroethene; *trans*-DCE, *trans*-1,2-dichloroethene; VC, vinyl chloride; 1,1,1-TCA, 1,1,1-trichloroethane; 1,1-DCA, 1,1-dichloroethane; CA, chloroethane; 1,1-DCE, 1,1-dichloroethene; total BTEX, sum of benzene, toluene, ethylbenzene, and xylene; total CVOCs, sum of chlorinated volatile organic compounds. **Abbreviations:** E, estimated value; M, presence verified but not quantified; μg/L, microgram per liter; dup, duplicate; blank, field blank; <, actual value is less than value shown; ND, not detected; –, not analyzed]

Well or piezometer No.	Date sampled	1,1,1-TCA (μg/L)	1,1-DCA (μg/L)	CA (μg/L)	1,1-DCE (μg/L)	Total BTEX (μg/L)	Total CVOCs (μg/L)
				Southern plantation—Continued			
MW1-5	06-22-00	–	–	–	–	–	–
	06-18-04	<1.0	E0.36	3.0	<1.0	E0.92	E1.6
	06-13-06	–	–	–	–	–	–
	06-20-07	–	–	–	–	–	–
	06-18-08	–	–	–	–	–	–
MW1-16	06-22-00	–	–	–	–	–	–
	06-22-04	<10	590	290	<10	367	890
	06-13-06	–	–	–	–	–	–
	06-20-07	–	–	–	–	–	–
	06-18-08	–	–	–	–	–	–
P1-6	06-08-99	<400	1,500	300	<400	E87	23,000
	06-14-01	<20	4,800	600	12	88	32,000
	06-13-02	<20	4,300	1,400	<20	63	15,000
	06-20-03	<50	380	270	<50	ND	3,600
	06-18-04	<20	200	88	<20	ND	1,100
	06-22-05	<130	370	400	<130	ND	8,000
	06-13-06	<100	1,200	2,600	<100	E68	5,000
	06-20-07	<8.0	69	78	<8.0	E1.4	380
	06-18-08	<200	400	1,200	<200	E46	20,000
P1-7	06-08-99	<670	<670	<1,300	<670	ND	64,000
	06-22-00	.24	17	8.4	72		75,000
	06-14-01	<20	<20	<20	44	ND	67,000
	06-14-02	<20	14	<20	64	ND	105,000
	06-20-03	<2,000	<2,000	<4,000	<2,000	ND	66,000
	06-18-04	<3,300	<3,300	<6,700	<3,300	ND	103,000
	06-22-05	<2,000	<2,000	<4,000	<2,000	ND	92,000
	06-13-06	<2,000	<2,000	<4,000	<2,000	ND	71,000
	06-20-07	<2,000	<2,000	<4,000	<2,000	ND	81,000
	06-18-08	<2,000	<2,000	<4,000	<2,000	ND	117,000
P1-8	06-07-99	<710	<710	<1,400	<710	ND	29,000
	06-14-01	<20	<20	<20	<20	ND	14,000
	06-13-02	<20	<20	<20	16	ND	32,000
	06-20-03	<10	E4	<20	<10	ND	270
	06-18-04	<1.0	<1.0	<2.0	<1.0	ND	26
	06-23-05	<1.0	<1.0	<2.0	<1.0	ND	28
	06-13-06	<20	<20	<40	<20	ND	680
	06-20-07	<4.0	<4.0	<8.0	<4.0	ND	72
	06-18-08	<10	<10	<20	<10	ND	440

Table 3. Concentrations of selected volatile organic compounds in groundwater samples from monitoring wells and piezometers collected by the U.S. Geological Survey at Operable Unit 1, Naval Undersea Warfare Center, Division Keyport, Washington, 1999–2008. —Continued

[All data except those shaded were published previously in Dinicola and others (2002), Dinicola (2003), Dinicola (2004), and Dinicola and Huffman (2004). Laboratory data qualifier codes, such as "D" for dilution, are not shown. **Volatile organic compounds (VOCs)**; PCE, tetrachloroethene; TCE, trichloroethene; *cis*-DCE, *cis*-1,2-dichloroethene; *trans*-DCE, *trans*-1,2-dichloroethene; VC, vinyl chloride; 1,1,1-TCA, 1,1,1-trichloroethane; 1,1-DCA, 1,1-dichloroethane; CA, chloroethane; 1,1-DCE, 1,1-dichloroethene; total BTEX, sum of benzene, toluene, ethylbenzene, and xylene; total CVOCs, sum of chlorinated volatile organic compounds. **Abbreviations:** E, estimated value; M, presence verified but not quantified; µg/L, microgram per liter; dup, duplicate; blank, field blank; <, actual value is less than value shown; ND, not detected; –, not analyzed]

Well or piezometer No.	Date sampled	PCE (µg/L)	TCE (µg/L)	*cis*-DCE (µg/L)	*trans*-DCE (µg/L)	VC (µg/L)	Ethane (µg/L)	Ethene (µg/L)
				Southern plantation—Continued				
P1-9	06-08-99	<2,000	48,000	88,000	470	7,200	–	–
	06-22-00	E5.0	88,000	64,000	320	5,800	–	37
	06-14-01	<40	29,000	7,300	32	450	–	–
	06-13-02	<20	90,000	79,000	590	7,900	–	–
	06-20-03	<1,000	60,000	27,000	<1,000	1,800	–	–
	06-18-04	<1,300	50,000	23,000	<1,300	2,100	16	200
	06-23-05	<20	230	700	E3.2	97	<5.0	E4.0
	06-13-06	<5,000	74,000	140,000	E850	10,000	66	1,200
	06-20-07	<1,000	55,000	40,000	E200	4,200	32	340
	06-18-08	<400	9700	13,000	E80	2,000	12	160
P1-10	06-07-99	<1,000	14,000	34,000	270	2,500	–	–
	06-22-00	1.0	8,700	13,000	100	2,300	–	2.3
	06-13-01	<20	6,600	12,000	68	1,800	–	–
	06-12-02	<20	4,600	7,000	55	2,000	–	–
	06-19-03	<400	2,300	9,400	<400	1,100	–	–
	06-18-04	<200	1,600	3,900	<200	890	E12	E46
	06-23-05	<100	1,100	3,000	E29	700	E3.0	7.0
	06-13-06	<1,000	2,200	27,000	E160	2,500	E19	E53
	06-20-07	<500	1,500	14,000	E130	1,700	E24	E34
	06-18-08	<200	490	5,800	E60	1,100	E20	E23
				Intermediate aquifer				
MW1-25	06-22-00	–	–	–	–	–	–	5.8
	06-14-02	<20	276	1,830	31	278	–	–
	06-19-03	<67	E14	1,800	E34	210	–	–
	06-16-04	–	–	–	–	–	E5.0	E15
	06-21-05	<67	<67	1,700	E30	220	E6.0	E13
	06-14-06	–	–	–	–	–	E7.0	E14
	06-18-07	–	–	–	–	–	E4.0	E8.1
	06-17-08	<50	<50	1,700	E28	510	E9.0	E15
MW1-28	06-22-00	–	–	–	–	–	–	2.6
	06-14-02	<20	69	1,600	72	700	–	–
	06-19-03	<50	<50	1,200	68	470	–	–
	06-16-04	–	–	–	–	–	E4.0	26
	06-21-05	<67	<67	1,500	84	650	E4.0	E22
	06-14-06	–	–	–	–	–	<50	E18
	06-18-07	–	–	–	–	–	E3.0	E15
	06-17-08	<50	<50	1,400	64	930	E6.0	28

Table 3   37

Table 3. Concentrations of selected volatile organic compounds in groundwater samples from monitoring wells and piezometers collected by the U.S. Geological Survey at Operable Unit 1, Naval Undersea Warfare Center, Division Keyport, Washington, 1999–2008. —Continued

[All data except those shaded were published previously in Dinicola and others (2002), Dinicola (2003), Dinicola (2004), and Dinicola and Huffman (2004). Laboratory data qualifier codes, such as "D" for dilution, are not shown. **Volatile organic compounds (VOCs)**; PCE, tetrachloroethene; TCE, trichloroethene; *cis*-DCE, *cis*-1,2-dichloroethene; *trans*-DCE, *trans*-1,2-dichloroethene; VC, vinyl chloride; 1,1,1-TCA, 1,1,1-trichloroethane; 1,1-DCA, 1,1-dichloroethane; CA, chloroethane; 1,1-DCE, 1,1-dichloroethene; total BTEX, sum of benzene, toluene, ethylbenzene, and xylene; total CVOCs, sum of chlorinated volatile organic compounds. **Abbreviations:** E, estimated value; M, presence verified but not quantified; µg/L, microgram per liter; dup, duplicate; blank, field blank; <, actual value is less than value shown; ND, not detected; –, not analyzed]

Well or piezometer No.	Date sampled	1,1,1-TCA (µg/L)	1,1-DCA (µg/L)	CA (µg/L)	1,1-DCE (µg/L)	Total BTEX (µg/L)	Total CVOCs (µg/L)
			Southern plantation—Continued				
P1-9	06-08-99	<2,000	<2,000	<4,000	<2,000	ND	144,000
	06-22-00	<10	E2.6	<20	47		158,000
	06-14-01	<40	<40	<40	<40	ND	37,000
	06-13-02	<20	<20	<20	54	11	178,000
	06-20-03	<1,000	<1,000	<2,000	<1,000	ND	89,000
	06-18-04	<1,300	<1,300	<2,700	<1,300	ND	75,000
	06-23-05	<20	<20	<40	<20	ND	1,000
	06-13-06	<5,000	<5,000	<10,000	<5,000	ND	225,000
	06-20-07	<1,000	<1,000	<2,000	<1,000	ND	99,000
	06-18-08	<400	<400	<800	<400	ND	25,000
P1-10	06-07-99	<1,000	<1,000	<2,000	<1,000	ND	51,000
	06-22-00	<.10	1.2	E.10	16		24,000
	06-13-01	<20	<20	<20	11	ND	20,000
	06-12-02	<20	<20	<20	<20	ND	14,000
	06-19-03	<400	<400	<800	<400	ND	13,000
	06-18-04	<200	<200	<400	<200	ND	6,400
	06-23-05	<100	<100	<200	<100	ND	4,800
	06-13-06	<1,000	<1,000	<2,000	<1,000	ND	32,000
	06-20-07	<500	<500	<1,000	<500	ND	17,000
	06-18-08	<200	<200	<400	<200	ND	7,400
			Intermediate aquifer				
MW1-25	06-22-00	–	–	–	–	–	–
	06-14-02	<20	<20	<20	<20	ND	2,400
	06-19-03	<67	<67	<130	<67	ND	2,100
	06-16-04	–	–	–	–	–	–
	06-21-05	<67	<67	<130	<67	ND	1,900
	06-14-06	–	–	–	–	–	–
	06-18-07	–	–	–	–	–	–
	06-17-08	<50	<50	<100	<50	ND	2,200
MW1-28	06-22-00	–	–	–	–	–	–
	06-14-02	<20	<20	<20	<20	ND	2,400
	06-19-03	<50	<50	<100	<50	ND	1,700
	06-16-04	–	–	–	–	–	–
	06-21-05	<67	<67	<130	<67	ND	2,200
	06-14-06	–	–	–	–	–	–
	06-18-07	–	–	–	–	–	–
	06-17-08	<50	<50	<100	<50	ND	2,400

Table 3. Concentrations of selected volatile organic compounds in groundwater samples from monitoring wells and piezometers collected by the U.S. Geological Survey at Operable Unit 1, Naval Undersea Warfare Center, Division Keyport, Washington, 1999–2008. —Continued

[All data except those shaded were published previously in Dinicola and others (2002), Dinicola (2003), Dinicola (2004), and Dinicola and Huffman (2004). Laboratory data qualifier codes, such as "D" for dilution, are not shown. **Volatile organic compounds (VOCs)**; PCE, tetrachloroethene; TCE, trichloroethene; *cis*-DCE, *cis*-1,2-dichloroethene; *trans*-DCE, *trans*-1,2-dichloroethene; VC, vinyl chloride; 1,1,1-TCA, 1,1,1-trichloroethane; 1,1-DCA, 1,1-dichloroethane; CA, chloroethane; 1,1-DCE, 1,1-dichloroethene; total BTEX, sum of benzene, toluene, ethylbenzene, and xylene; total CVOCs, sum of chlorinated volatile organic compounds. **Abbreviations:** E, estimated value; M, presence verified but not quantified; µg/L, microgram per liter; dup, duplicate; blank, field blank; <, actual value is less than value shown; ND, not detected; –, not analyzed]

Well or piezometer No.	Date sampled	PCE (µg/L)	TCE (µg/L)	*cis*-DCE (µg/L)	*trans*-DCE (µg/L)	VC (µg/L)	Ethane (µg/L)	Ethene (µg/L)
				Intermediate aquifer—Continued				
MW1-38	06-20-00	–	–	–	–	–	–	0.57
	06-12-02	<0.20	<0.20	<0.20	<0.20	<0.20	–	–
	06-16-04	–	–	–	–	–	<5.0	<5.0
	06-24-05	<1.0	<1.0	<1.0	<1.0	<1.0	<5.0	<5.0
	06-14-06	–	–	–	–	–	<5.0	<5.0
	06-21-07	–	–	–	–	–	<5.0	<5.0
	06-17-08	–	–	–	–	–	M	<5.0
MW1-39	06-07-99	<1.0	<1.0	0.30	<0.50	1.0	–	–
	06-20-00	–	–	–	–	–	–	0.26
	06-12-01	–	–	–	–	–	–	–
	06-12-02	–	–	–	–	–	–	–
	06-19-03	<1.0	<1.0	E.60	<1.0	1.0	–	–
	06-16-04	–	–	–	–	–	<5.0	<5.0
	06-14-06	–	–	–	–	–	<50	<50
	06-21-07	–	–	–	–	–	<25	<25
	06-17-08	<1.0	<1.0	E.53	<1.0	3.0	<20	<20

Table 3   39

Table 3.   Concentrations of selected volatile organic compounds in groundwater samples from monitoring wells and piezometers collected by the U.S. Geological Survey at Operable Unit 1, Naval Undersea Warfare Center, Division Keyport, Washington, 1999–2008. —Continued

[All data except those shaded were published previously in Dinicola and others (2002), Dinicola (2003), Dinicola (2004), and Dinicola and Huffman (2004). Laboratory data qualifier codes, such as "D" for dilution, are not shown. **Volatile organic compounds (VOCs)**: PCE, tetrachloroethene; TCE, trichloroethene; *cis*-DCE, *cis*-1,2-dichloroethene; *trans*-DCE, *trans*-1,2-dichloroethene; VC, vinyl chloride; 1,1,1-TCA, 1,1,1-trichloroethane; 1,1-DCA, 1,1-dichloroethane; CA, chloroethane; 1,1-DCE, 1,1-dichloroethene; total BTEX, sum of benzene, toluene, ethylbenzene, and xylene; total CVOCs, sum of chlorinated volatile organic compounds. **Abbreviations:** E, estimated value; M, presence verified but not quantified; µg/L, microgram per liter; dup, duplicate; blank, field blank; <, actual value is less than value shown; ND, not detected; –, not analyzed]

Well or piezometer No.	Date sampled	1,1,1-TCA (µg/L)	1,1-DCA (µg/L)	CA (µg/L)	1,1-DCE (µg/L)	Total BTEX (µg/L)	Total CVOCs (µg/L)
				Intermediate aquifer—Continued			
MW1-38	06-20-00	–	–	–	–	–	–
	06-12-02	<0.20	<0.20	<0.20	<0.20	ND	ND
	06-16-04	–	–	–	–	–	–
	06-24-05	<1.0	<1.0	<2.0	<1.0	ND	ND
	06-14-06	–	–	–	–	–	–
	06-21-07	–	–	–	–	–	–
	06-17-08	–	–	–	–	–	–
MW1-39	06-07-99	<1.0	<1.0	<2.0	<1.0	ND	1.0
	06-20-00	–	–	–	–	–	–
	06-12-01	–	–	–	–	–	–
	06-12-02	–	–	–	–	–	–
	06-19-03	<1.0	<1.0	<2.0	<1.0	ND	1.6
	06-16-04	–	–	–	–	–	–
	06-14-06	–	–	–	–	–	–
	06-21-07	–	–	–	–	–	–
	06-17-08	<1.0	<1.0	<2.0	<1.0	ND	3.5

Appendix A. Quality Assurance and Control of U.S. Geological Survey 2007 and 2008 Geochemical Sampling

Quality assurance and control of geochemical sampling included the collection of duplicate and field blank samples for selected redox-sensitive analytes and Volatile Organic Compounds (VOCs). Field blanks were collected by pumping inorganic blank water and VOC-free water through new clean tubing to determine possible sampling contamination. Complete laboratory quality assurance and control data from TestAmerica (TA) Laboratories is on file with the U.S Geological Survey Washington Water Science Center in Tacoma, Washington.

Duplicate sample results compared favorably for all constituents (table A1). A duplicate sample was collected and analyzed by the National Water Quality Laboratory (NWQL) for organic carbon, manganese, nitrate and nitrite, sulfate, chloride, ethene, and ethane for well MW1-38 and piezometers P1-4 and P1-9. The duplicate results for these constituents agreed within 13 percent. Duplicate samples were collected and analyzed for VOCs at piezometers P1-4 and P1-9 and the concentrations agreed within 30 percent (table A1).

Filtered chloride was detected at an estimated concentration of 0.06 mg/L in the blank sample collected in 2007 (MW1-38), which is small compared to filtered chloride concentrations in environmental samples that were measured at 4.3 mg/L or higher. Dissolved organic carbon was detected at the method reporting limit concentration of 0.40 mg/L in the blank sample collected in 2008 (associated with site 1MW-1). Chloroethenes, chloroethanes, and benzene, toluene, ethylbenze, were not detected in the field blank samples (associated with wells MW1-38 and 1MW-1). Xylene was detected at an estimated concentration of 0.48 µg/L in the field blank sample in 2007 (MW1-38), which is comparable in magnitude to many total BTEX concentrations in environmental samples. No ethene, ethane, or chloroethene, or choroethane compounds of interest were detected in the laboratory method blanks. No changes were made to the dataset based on these quality control data.

Table A1.   Quality assurance data collected by the U.S. Geological Survey at Operable Unit 1, Naval Undersea Warfare Center, Division Keyport, Washington, June 2007 and June 2008.

[**Well or piezometer No.:** D denotes duplicate sample; FB denotes field blank sample. **Volatile organic compounds (VOCs):** PCE, tetrachloroethene; TCE, trichloroethene; *cis*-DCE, *cis*-1,2-dichloroethene; *trans*-DCE, *trans*-1,2-dichloroethene; VC, vinyl chloride; TCA, 1,1,-trichloroethane; 1,1-DCA, 1,1-dichloroethane, CA, chloroethane; 1,1-DCE, 1,1-dichloroethene; BTEX, benzene, toluene, ethylbezene, and xylene; CVOCs, sum of all chloroethenes and chloroethane concentrations shown in table. **Abbreviations:** mg/L, milligrams per liter; nd, not detected; µg/L, micrograms per liter; nd, not detected. **Symbols:** <, actual value is less than the value shown; –, not analyzed]

Well or piezometer No.	Date sampled	PCE (µ/L)	TCE (µg/L)	*cis*-DCE (µg/L)	*trans*-DCE (µg/L)	VC (µg/L)	Ethane (µg/L)	Ethene (µg/L)	111-TCA (µg/L)	1,1-DCA (µg/L)	CA (µg/L)	1,1-DCE (µg/L)
P1-4	06-19-07	<40	<40	1,500	24	280	E11	E29	<40	<40	<80	<40
P1-4D	06-19-07	<80	E44	2,400	E28	470	E10	E28	<80	<80	<160	<80
MW1-38FB	06-21-07	<1.0	<1.0	<1.0	<1.0	<1.0	–	–	<1.0	<1.0	<2.0	<1.0
MW1-38	06-17-08	–	–	–	–	–	–	–	–	–	–	–
MW1-38D	06-17-08	–	–	–	–	–	–	–	–	–	–	–
MW1-5	06-18-08	–	–	–	–	–	E7.0	<50	–	–	–	–
MW1-5D	06-18-08	–	–	–	–	–	E6.0	E8.1	–	–	–	–
P1-9	06-18-08	<400	9,700	13,000	E80	2,000	12	160	<400	<400	<800	<400
P1-9D	06-18-08	<800	12,000	16,000	<800	2,700	11	150	<800	<800	<1,600	<800
1MW-1FB	06-18-08	<1.0	<1.0	<1.0	<1.0	<2.0	–	–	<1.0	<1.0	<2.0	<1.0

Well or piezometer No.	Date sampled	Total		Dissolved oxygen (mg/L)	Filtered NO$_2$ + NO$_3$ (mg/L)	Filtered (dissolved) organic carbon (mg/L)	Filtered manga-nese (mg/L)	Filtered iron (II) (mg/L)	Filtered sulfate (mg/L)	Unfiltered sulfide (mg/L)	Dissolved methane (mg/L)	Dissolved carbon dioxide (mg/L)	Filtered chloride (mg/L)
		BTEX (µg/L)	CVOCs (µg/L)										
P1-4	06-19-07	66	1,800	<0.1	<0.06	7.1	0.35	3.2	4.70	<0.01	2,500	26	43
P1-4D	06-19-07	ND	3,000	<.01	<.06	7.4	.35	3.1	4.78	<.01	2,600	29	43
MW1-38FB	06-21-07	0.48	ND	–	<.06	<.40	<.20	–	<.18	–	–	–	E.06
MW1-38	06-17-08	–	–	.1	<.04	5.0	.04	.03	2.51	.02	620	<10	230
MW1-38D	06-17-08	–	–	.1	<.04	5.1	.04	.03	2.69	.02	–	<10	220
MW1-5	06-18-08	–	–	–	–	–	–	–	–	–	1,800	–	–
MW1-5D	06-18-08	–	–	–	–	–	–	–	–	–	1,600	–	–
P1-9	06-18-08	ND	25,000	<.1	<.04	10.5	.17	.07	7.89	<.01	740	<10	28
P1-9D	06-18-08	ND	31,000	<.1	<.04	11.4	.16	.07	8.04	<.01	730	<10	26
1MW-1FB	06-18-08	–	–	–	–	.40	–	–	–	–	–	–	–

www.ingramcontent.com/pod-product-compliance
Lightning Source LLC
Chambersburg PA
CBHW080344290526
45791CB00009BA/2733